CFA Level 1 Financial Statement Analysis

CFA level 1, Volume 1

M. Imran Ahsan

Published by M. Imran Ahsan, 2024.

While every precaution has been taken in the preparation of this book, the publisher assumes no responsibility for errors or omissions, or for damages resulting from the use of the information contained herein.

CFA LEVEL 1 FINANCIAL STATEMENT ANALYSIS

First edition. August 31, 2024.

Copyright © 2024 M. Imran Ahsan.

ISBN: 979-8223373452

Written by M. Imran Ahsan.

Also by M. Imran Ahsan

ACCA
AACA: Business & Technology

CFA level 1
CFA 2025: Level 1 corporate Issuers
CFA Level 1 Financial Statement Analysis
CFA level 1: 2025 Equity Investments
CFA 2025: Level 1 Fixed Income
Economics for CFA 2024: level 1 in just one week
CFA Level 1: Derivatives and Alternative Investments
CFA 2025: level 1 Portfolio management

Investment series
Corporate Finance: A Beginner's Guide
Fixed Income Securities: A Beginner's Guide to Understand, Invest
and Evaluate Fixed Income Securities

To all Smart learners

Financial Statement Analysis 2024-2025

Learning Module 1
Introduction to Financial Statement Analysis

1: Describe the steps in the financial statement analysis framework
Following is a six-step basic framework for financial analysis.

1. Articulate the purpose and the context of the analysis
2. Collect data
3. Process the data
4. Analyze and interpret the data
5. Develop reports and communicate the conclusions
6. Follow up/update the analysis

1. Articulate the purpose and the context of the analysis:
First of all, we need to articulate what is the purpose of our analysis. An analyst might be working on different perspectives to evaluate a company. These perspectives might include

Evaluation of a company as an equity investment, Potential acquisition, analysis of the company`s creditworthiness, or any other intentions given by the client.

2. Collect data: At this stage, all the sources of information, like financial statements, management`s commentary, conference calls, etc., are needed to collect the data about a company.

3. Process the data: At this stage, all the data collected in the previous stage is processed. We might be calculating financial ratios and common size statements, building models or forecasting etc.

4. Analyze and interpret the data: At this stage, we start to build an assessment of the company. We answer the questions we were looking for in first stage.

5. Develop reports and communicate the conclusions: At this stage, we draw conclusions, develop a report, and communicate it with the intended audience/client. The report must comply with Codes and Standards.

6. Follow up/update the analysis: At this stage we gather and update our previously collected data/information and update our conclusions. Updating might include repetition of some previous steps.

2: Describe the roles of financial statement analysis

Financial reporting: These are the methods a firm/company uses to explain its financial position and health.

The management prepares unaudited and audited financial statements for the general public and the users of financial statements. The financial statements include income statements, balance sheets, statements of cash flow, and other financial disclosures required by regulatory bodies/accounting standard-setting bodies.

The users of financial statements are those who make economic decisions based on these reports, such as investors, lenders, company management, government, analysts, etc.

Financial statements analysis is about evaluating company performance using these published financial reports. The information in the statements and disclosures is used by analysts to evaluate the company`s current and past performance to make an opinion about the firm, like whether or not we should invest in this company. A bank can also think of whether or not they should pass the loan application of this particular company.

3: Describe the importance of regulatory filings, financial statement notes and supplementary information, management's commentary, and audit reports

There are two major company`s financial disclosures

Footnotes

The management's discussion and analysis.

The footnotes: The footnotes to the financial statements help us to understand the company`s position and performance. They give us information about the company`s fiscal year, standards used in the preparation of financial statements, accounting assumptions, insight about unique transactions and legal proceedings, employee benefit plans, contingencies and commitments, acquisitions, and disposals of businesses and segments of the firm. (We will discuss all of these later).

Management`s commentary: Also known as the management's discussion and analysis (MD&A), management's report, operating and financial review.

This is also a very crucial source of information for an analyst to understand financial reports. One thing to remember here, the MD&A is generally unaudited.

IFRS guidelines suggest the following information in this section,

Nature of the business, management objectives, company's past performance, current business environment and future outlook, the performance measures used, the company's essential relationships, resources owned by the company, and risks.

<u>US GAAP requires that MD&A must include</u>

❖ Significant Events and future uncertainties which will affect liquidity, capital resources and main operations of the firm.

❖ Inflation and off-balance sheet items, obligations like purchase /sale agreements, or any other contractual agreement.

❖ Accounting policies are based on management`s judgment.

❖ Other important sources of information are Securities and Exchange Commission filings like

Form 8-K: Under Form 8 K, the companies are required to disclose

Acquisitions and disposals of major assets

Changes in management or corporate governance.

This form is submitted when changes occur, so this is a very important one.

Quarterly financial statements are filed under **Form 10-Q.** This also includes any material changes in business and any new information regarding the company`s management.

Form 10-k: It is filed with audited annual reports and information about the business, management, and legal matters.

Proxy statements: When matters require shareholder`s votes this statement is issued to them. These are matters like the election of the board of directors, their compensation, etc.

Audit: An audit is the inspection of financial statements and supporting documents by an independent body (an auditor or body of auditors).

Objective of audit: The objective of the audit is to create an opinion about the fairness and reliability of a set of financial statements and documents.

4: Describe implications for financial analysis of alternative financial reporting systems and the importance of monitoring developments in financial reporting standards

As Accounting standards continuously evolve, an analyst must remain updated about these changes and innovations. Analysts must visit professional journals, the IASB website (www.ifrs.org), and the FASB website (www.fasb.org). CFA Institute also issues position papers on financial reporting issues.

Analysts must also check for the company's disclosures for accounting standards used, accounting policies, and estimates.

5: Describe information sources that analysts use in financial statement analysis besides annual and interim financial reports

We know that companies must issue annual reports to show their financial results and performances. In the meantime, companies also release quarterly and semiannual reports, which analysts must consider while evaluating the performance of the company. These interim reports (generally unaudited) and their footnotes are a vital source of information to an analyst because these statements show major financial events during that interim.

Other important sources of information are Securities and Exchange Commission filings like

Form 8-K: Under Form 8 K, the companies are required to disclose Acquisitions and disposals of major assets

Changes in management or corporate governance.

This form is submitted when changes occur, so this is a very important one.

Quarterly financial statements are filed under Form 10-Q. This also includes any material changes in business and any new information regarding the company's management.

Form 10-k is filed with audited annual reports and information about the business, management, and legal matters.

Proxy statements: When there are matters which require shareholder's votes this statement is issued to them. These are matters like the election of the board of directors, their compensation, etc.

Sources of information other than SEC filings;

Press releases and corporate reports: Companies often release these items. They can be a source of information up to some extent.

Conference calls: This is another important source for an analyst. After earnings are announced, senior management answers the questions in a conference call.

Earnings guidance is given by the management to present its own performance expectations.

Industry reports: the reports of the industry and especially the competitors are also good sources of information.

Analysts must also consider the economic conditions of businesses and countries in analyzing the companies. He/she can get more information from economic and business journals, statistical journals, and the government journals.

Learning Module 2
Analyzing Income Statements

1: Describe general principles of revenue recognition, specific revenue recognition applications, and implications of revenue recognition choices for financial analysis

Remember, revenues do not depend upon cash. When goods are sold on credit, revenue is recognized when;

❖ Ownership of the goods changes hands from selling to buying party.
❖ When the risk and reward of owning goods has moved to a buying party.

With IFRS, we must recognize revenues in the sale of goods under the following conditions.

- When the risk and reward of owning goods has moved to a buying party.
- The selling party has no managerial influence/control over the goods.
- The expected revenue can be reliably measured.
- It is likely and probable that the economic benefit of the transaction will flow to the selling entity.
- The cost of the transaction can be reliably measured.

In case of the delivery of services, the following conditions are followed

- The expected revenue can be reliably measured.
- It is likely and probable that the economic benefits of transactions will flow to the selling party.

- The cost of the transaction can be measured.
- The stage of the completion of the transaction must be reliably measured.

With GAAP, revenue must be recognized if it is

Realized, realizable, or earned.

These are some special cases in which revenue recognition becomes more difficult.

Exceptional cases can be

- long-term contracts
- Installment sales.
- Barter transactions.
- The gross and net reporting of revenue.

Long-term contracts: Long-term contracts mean revenue streams will cover multiple accounting periods (more than one year).

The issue is when we recognize the revenue. If we recognize it when the contract occurred, that will exaggerate reported income in the current period, and the income for subsequent years will be underweight.

So, we need to divide the overall revenue amount across multiple years, maybe an equal or prorated (unequal) distribution across each year, or maybe recognition should be based on our understanding of the underlying business circumstances using a method called

Percentage of completion

It estimates the percentage of the contract that is complete. If the contract is 60 % complete, then the company should recognize 60 % of the revenue up to that point. We calculate the percentage of project completion by calculating the percentage of total cost we have spent.

For example, a company has entered into a project which will take five years to complete.

Total cost of the project is estimated = $20 million

The price at which it will be sold =$30 m.

In the first year, we spent 5 million, which is 25 percent of the overall cost.

So, the 25% of total revenues (25% of 30 m) should be reported for the first year and the same method for the next years.

If the outcome of the project is not actually known at the beginning (of long-term contract)

IFRS and U. S. GAAP differ in this circumstance.

Under IFRS, as long as we have sufficient incoming revenue to justify the level of spending, we can recognize revenue to the extent of the costs incurred. It means revenues =costs. Profit is only recognized at completion.

Under US GAAP, we use the completed contract method. The project doesn't go to the income statement at all. Only loss is recognized immediately. The cumulative cost is recorded on the balance sheet, where cash goes down as it is spent. And some other assets (inventory) are rising as the project is on its way to being completed. In the final year, we record total revenue and total cost. In years other than final, we do not recognize any cost or revenues under US GAAP.

Installment sales (Another long-term contract)

This situation is where sales proceeds will be received in installments over multiple periods.

Under IFRS, the expected installment payments are discounted back to their present value. That discounted amount is then recognized on the date of the sale as the sales price. The remainder, the difference between the simple sum of payments and the present value of those payments, will be recognized over time as an interest component.

Under U.S GAAP, we have two methods

Installment method

Cost recovery method

Let's understand these two with the help of an example.

Let's say a company is selling one of its plants.

The plant cost was $5m, and they agreed on a price of $8m. The buying party has offered a down payment of $1.5m, and the remaining $6.5 m will be paid over a period of 10 years.

Under the installment method, a portion of the profit is recognized as being in line with the percentage of the total sales price, which is profit.

In our case, the total profit is $3 m, which is 37.5 % of total deal value ($8m)

Then, we take 37.5 % of the down payment (1.5 m) to get a profit attributable to the down payment of $562500.

And whenever we receive cash its 37.5 percent will be recognized as profit, and the remaining is cost.

Cost recovery method: In this method, profit cannot be recorded until the amount of cash is greater than the initial cost, so because the cash amount paid by the buyer is not higher than the original cost, no profit would be recorded unless when the cash amount supersedes the cost it will be recorded as profit in coming periods.

Barter transactions:

Let's say two companies exchanging advertising space. This means that they are exchanging assets or services that are very similar to each other.

So, there should be very little or no effect on income.

Under IFRS, revenue can be recognized from this type of transaction in an amount equal to that from a similar non-barter transaction between unrelated parties.

Under US GAAP, we can only recognize revenue from barter transactions if we have previously recognized cash for a similar transaction.

Revenue Recognition Steps

There are five steps involved in recognizing revenue:

❖ Identify the contract (or contracts) pertaining to a customer

❖ Identify performance obligations in the contract

❖ Determine the transaction price (or prices)

❖ Allocate the transaction price (or prices) to the performance obligations in each contract

❖ Recognize revenue whenever the entity satisfies a performance obligation.

Choice of revenue recognition method

Typically, firms buy products and/or raw materials from their suppliers and sell them to their customers. So, the cost of goods sold and revenues are easily distinguishable.

With E. business, companies were selling products that they never purchased or manufactured. They simply take in the revenue and then arrange delivery directly from the supplier to the customer.

The question is, should they be reporting revenue in the total amount received from the customer (called gross revenue reporting) or their earnings only (called net revenues reporting) since earnings are more like a commission as the spread between the amount they have received in the cost of them from the supplier.

Under U. S. GAAP: If the following conditions are fulfilled, the firm can report gross revenues otherwise net revenues.

- If the selling company is the primary under a contract.
- If they bear inventory risk and credit risk.
- If they have more than one supplier.
- They have a reasonable influence over the price.

2: Describe general principles of expense recognition, specific expense recognition applications, implications of expense recognition choices for financial analysis and contrast costs that are capitalized versus those that are expensed in the period in which they are incurred

Expenses: The IASB Conceptual Framework describes expenses as "decreases in economic benefits during the accounting period in the form of outflows or depletions of assets or increase in liabilities that result in a decrease in equity, other than those relating to distributions to equity participants."

General Principles of Expense Recognition: A company recognizes expenses when it consumes the economic benefits associated with the expenditure or loses some previously recognized economic benefit.

Matching principle: Under the matching principle, a company recognizes some expenses (for example, cost of goods sold) whenever the associated revenues are recognized. Matching requires that a company recognize the cost of goods sold in the same period as revenues from the sale of the goods. Matching is applied to inventory and the cost of goods sold.

Period costs are expenditures that directly match revenue and are reflected in the period when a company has the expenditure or incurs a liability. For example, administrative expenses.

Specific identification method, the inventory, and the cost of goods sold are based on their physical flow. IFRS and US GAAP, however, permit the use of the first in, first out (FIFO) method and the weighted average cost method to assign costs.

FIFO method: In this method, the oldest goods that are purchased /manufactured are sold first, while the newest goods purchased or manufactured remain in inventory. So, the ending inventory would include the most recent purchases.

Weighted average cost method: In this method, the average costs of goods available for sale are assigned to the units sold and those remaining in inventory.

Last in, first out (LIFO) method: This method is only allowed under US GAAP, but IFRS does not permit it. Under this method, the newest goods purchased /manufactured are sold first, while the oldest goods purchased/manufactured remain in inventory. So, the costs of the latest items purchased will flow into the costs of goods sold first.

Specific Expense Recognition Applications

Doubtful accounts: While using the matching principle, once revenue is recognized, a company must record an estimate of uncollectible revenues. This estimate is recorded as an uncollectable reserve/ reserve for doubtable debts (an expense) on the income statement, not deducted from revenues directly.

Warranties: While recognizing revenues from sales of warrantable goods and or services, companies are required to estimate the amount of future expenses that might result from these warranties to recognize estimated warranty expenses in the periods of sale (not at a later date).

Depreciation and Amortization: Depreciation is the process of systematically allocating the costs of long-lived assets over their useful life. There are many methods for computing depreciation. These are the straight-line method, the diminishing balance method, and the units of production method.

Straight-line method: Under this method, the cost of long-lived assets less the estimated residual value is allocated evenly over the asset's estimated useful life.

Annual Depreciation under the straight-line method = (Cost-residual value)/ (Useful life)

Example: ABS Company purchases machinery at a cost of $10 m. They expect to use it for 10 years, after which they will sell it for $1m. Calculate annual depreciation using the straight-line method.

Solution: We know the formula for the straight-line method, Annual Depreciation under the straight-line method = (Cost-residual value)/ (Useful life)

By putting values in our formula, we got annual depreciation = (10m-1m)/10 =900000$

The diminishing balance method and the units of production methods are referred to as accelerated methods of depreciation because they accelerate the timing of depreciation by allocating a greater proportion of the depreciation expense to the early years of an asset's useful life.

Amortization Expense Recognition

The term amortization is used whenever the long-lived assets are intangible and have a finite, useful life. Amortization expense should match the proportion of the asset's benefits used during the period. Many firms use the straight-line method to calculate annual amortization expense. Straight-line amortization is exactly like straight-line depreciation. Intangible assets with indefinite lives, like goodwill (not amortized), must be annually tested for impairment. If these items are impaired, the impairment amount is an expense that must be included in the income statement as an expense.

Implications of Expense Recognition Choices for Financial Analysis

The choice of depreciation or amortization method and the estimate of useful life and residual value can affect a company's reported net income. Also, the company's estimates for doubtful debts and warranty expenses affect net income.

An analyst, familiar with the monetary effects of different expense recognition policies and estimates, can efficiently compare different companies or within a single company's historical performance. These effects may be used to adjust for better comparison.

3: Describe the financial reporting treatment and analysis of non-recurring items (including discontinued operations, unusual or infrequent items) and changes in accounting policies

When evaluating a company's future earnings, it essential to separate incomes and expenses that are likely to continue in the future from those that are less likely to continue.

IFRS and U. S. GAAP do offer some guidelines to separate them, but some items have less clear future and require some judgment from analysts. *We are going to look in*

1. Discontinued operations
2. Extraordinary items.
3. Unusual or infrequent items.
4. Changes in accounting policies
5. Operating versus non-operating items.

A discontinued operation is a part of the business being disposed of. It means that part will not play any role in the future.

US GAAP and IFRS require this to be reported separately in the income statement as a discontinued operation. Since that part of the business will not drive revenue in the future, it is eliminated when developing a forecast.

Extraordinary Items: Items of income and expense that are considered both infrequent and unusual are considered extraordinary.

This classification is not permitted under IFRS. After December 2015, US GAAP also does not permit this classification. But before December 2015 under U. S. GAAP this classification existed.

Unusual or infrequent items: These are reported before tax with continued operations.

Items that are considered in this category include

- Sale of the business unit at a considerable premium (gains) or discount (losses).

- Gains or losses from Impairments, write-offs, write-downs, and restructuring charges.

Under US GAAP, items that are either unusual or infrequent are not considered extraordinary; you need to be both unusual and infrequent for that classification.

For example, restructuring charges or selling the business unit at a considerable premium or discount. These items will be reported with the company's continuing operations.

Under IFRS, the accounting treatment is a bit different. Based on the idea that a single income or expense that is material or relevant to the understanding of the business should be reported separately, anything unusual or infrequent would have to be reported separately.

Changes in accounting policies:

The change in accounting policy could be of two types.

- A new accounting standard set up by the standard-setting authority or company decided to move from IFRS to GAAP or the other way around.
- Changes in accounting estimates

Changes in applicable accounting standards are required to be applied retrospectively. It means whenever a company changes its accounting standard, they are required to restate their previous financial statements according to new standards because it would be misleading for a company to be able to use two different sets of accounting standards on the same document side by side. (Use of LIFO is an exception here. We will discuss it under inventories in detail).

Change in an accounting estimate: The effect of a change in an accounting estimate is not required to be applied retrospectively. Because it depends upon the management's judgment, usually after getting new information.

For example, if the management realizes that some specific asset has a longer or shorter useful life than previously estimated. It will significantly change expense (depreciation), and it is required to be mentioned in the notes accompanying the statement.

<u>Analytical implications:</u>

In forecasting there is considerable judgment in the end of analyst is needed. The analyst must decide whether to include or remove any item from the analysis. The analyst must see whether or not new policies have effects on cash flow. If they have, more care is required at the end of the analysis to include or exclude items from the analysis. Changes in standards are disclosed, and the documents are restated according to new standards, so there is not much to worry about in this case.

4: Describe how earnings per share is calculated and calculate and interpret a company's basic and diluted earnings per share for companies with simple and complex capital structures including those with antidilutive securities

Simple and complex capital structure: If a company issues any financial instruments that can be converted into common stock, then we have a complex capital structure, and if not, it means we have a simple capital structure.

EPS stands for earnings per share, and basic EPS is just that. Basic EPS = company's earnings that are available for distribution to common stockholders / weighted average number of shares of common stock outstanding

Diluted EPS takes a company's complex capital structure into account.

<u>Basic and diluted EPS are the same if the company has a simple capital structure.</u>

Diluted EPS is a performance metric used to gauge the quality of a company's **earnings per share** (**EPS**) if all convertible securities were exercised (converted into common stock). If convertibles exist, they bring down the diluted EPS, down from basic EPS.

Dilutive and anti-dilutive securities:

Dilutive securities are those that bring up the number of shares outstanding in the calculation of diluted EPS and bring the EPS figure down.

Anti-dilutive securities are those that, if they were converted and included, would bring EPS up.

5: Evaluate a company's financial performance using common-size income statements and financial ratios based on the income statement

Common size analysis of the income statement:

When building a vertical common-size income statement, every item in the income statement is described as a percentage of revenue. (i.e. $\frac{\text{Cost of goods sold}}{\text{Revenues}} \times 100$)

By doing this, we eliminate the size effect and standardize the statement to facilitate comparison in terms of its past performance and also in comparison to other companies in the industry.

By combining common size analysis with profitability ratios, we can come up with some very quick insights into the company's performance.

Two major components of that analysis are the gross profit margin ($= \frac{\text{Gross profit}}{\text{Revenues}} \times 100$), and net profit margin Net profit margin$= \frac{\text{Net profit}}{\text{Revenues}} \times 100$.

Gross profit margin is generally an indicator of a company's strategy. Now, a higher GP margin indicates lower costs, which is desirable, but an analyst must analyze why a company is different from its peer group.

Are they using a new technology so their production procedure becomes more efficient than others?

<u>The net profit margin tells us how much money we earn</u> for every dollar of revenue. Several components can be manipulated to get higher NP. Analysts must consider them. Still, lower NP is not desirable.

Let's convert the income statement of ABC Corporation Ltd into common size

Sales	100 m
CGS	-20m
GP	80m
Admin expenses	-1m
Selling expenses	-1m
Net profit	78m

Common size income statement

Sales	$(100/100) \times 100 = 100\%$
CGS	$(20/100) \times 100 = 20\%$
GP	80%
Admin expenses	1%
Selling expenses	1%
Net profit	78%

Learning Module 3
Analyzing Balance Sheets

1: Explain the financial reporting and disclosures related to intangible assets

For companies reporting under IFRS, each of the following items must be disclosed for intangible assets.

⬦ The basis for measuring the asset's value (i.e., historical cost etc.),

⬦ Amortization method used,

⬦ Gross carrying value of asset, a reconciliation of any change in the asset's carrying value over the period,

⬦ Any restrictions related to the assets that are pledged as collateral and any agreements that you're currently in place for the future acquisition of assets.

⬦ Intangible asset's useful life is finite or indefinite, is required.

For impaired assets, we need to disclose

⬦ The amounts of any impairment write-downs or reversals.
⬦ Impacts of those write-downs and reversals on the income statement
⬦ Circumstances that brought about that impairment or reversal.

Firms that report under the cost model would follow the same guidelines as ordinary long-lived assets. Firms reporting using the fair

value model will be required to include additional disclosures related to the determination of fair value.

Under U. S. GAAP, the disclosure requirements are not as detailed. Companies must disclose the aggregate amortization expense amount, classified listing of growth carrying amounts, classified accumulated amortization figures, and the estimated amortization expense for the next five years.

Companies reporting under U. S. GAAP do not have the option of reversing impairments.

For impaired assets, the following disclosures are required under U. S. GAAP

◇ a description of the impaired assets,

◇ the circumstances that led to the impairment,

◇ the method used to determine the asset`s fair value,

◇ The amount of the impairment loss and the impact it has on the income statement.

2: Explain the financial reporting and disclosures related to goodwill

An asset that bears no physical substance and does not match the criteria of identifiable intangible assets.

One good example of an unidentifiable intangible asset is good-will, which is the excessive purchase price over the fair value of assets acquired.

Good-will: Good-will arises when a company acquires another company and pays more than the fair value of the acquired assets. Goodwill goes into the balance sheet as an asset and is tested annually and written down if impaired.

There is the problem of comparison between two companies, with one having grown by acquisition, and the other having grown internally. The acquiring firm records goodwill by capitalizing the extra payment on acquisition while the internally growing company normally has expensed its growth expenditures.

The cost of an asset with an indefinite life will not be amortized but will be tested annually for impairment.

If impairment occurs, then the asset's value will be written down on the balance sheet, and the firm report a loss on its income statement.

Accounting for intangibles depends on how they were acquired.

- Assets might be purchased.
- Developed internally.
- Or acquired as part of the business combination.

When an asset is purchased, the accounting treatment is similar to tangible long-lived assets.

The purchase price is assumed to be equal to fair value, and that's the figure used to record the asset on the balance sheet. Then

For assets that were developed internally, the accounting treatment is a bit different.

When an asset is purchased the company will have one easily identifiable transaction that can drive an asset being capitalized on the balance sheet.

Assets which are developed internally will have come about through a series of expenses the company would have recognized in the periods which they were incurred. The company will have spent money over time on a wide variety of expenses and it's the combination of all of these varying expenses that lead the company to own this intangible asset. So, the company will recognize a series of expenditures on their income statement over time. These together will develop into an intangible asset that they own.

A good example would be continuous expenditures on R & D program or an advertising or marketing plan.

Over time these might develop into a recognizable brand and brand recognition.

The differing accounting treatments we have seen here will spark a major difference between the financial statements of companies who purchase assets and those who have developed them internally.

On the one hand you have companies with assets on the balance sheet compared to companies that do not have assets to report. This is because companies who develop their assets internally have expensed their acquisition costs as they were being developed.

At the same time, you have these purchasing companies recognizing expenditures as investing cash flows. While the companies developing the assets are recognizing these expenses as operating cash flows.

Intangibles acquired as part of the business combination: Assets acquired through a business combination are accounted for using the acquisition methods. Assets acquired are recorded on the balance sheet of the acquirer at fair value. The difference between the overall purchase price and the combined amount attributable to the acquired assets is recorded as good will.

It's important to know that this is what we consider good will to be an on identifiable intangible asset. It cannot be separated from the acquired business.

3: Explain the financial reporting and disclosures related to financial instruments

According to IFRS, financial instruments are contracts that generate assets for one entity and liabilities, or equity for another organization. Financial instruments can be categorized as asset or liability depending on the nature of the contract. Bonds, equity stocks and nots are financial instruments.

Financial instruments are recognized when the company come under the contract.

These financial instruments are measured by either of the following was;

1. Amortized cost
2. Fair value

1. Financial instruments measured at amortized cost

The amortized cost of a financial asset (or liability) = initially recognized amount – principal re-payment – discounts + premium – any other reduction like impairment.

Under IFRS: If the financial assets are intended to be kept until maturity, and the cash flows from these instruments are predetermined and occur on certain dates, consisting only of principal payments and interest, these instruments are measured at amortized cost.

Under US GAAP: The instruments are measured at amortized cost if they are intended to be held till maturity, no matter the interest payments or cash flows fluctuate.

1. Financial instruments Measured at Fair Value

There are two methods for financial instruments to be recognized as fair value;

a. as profit or loss (unrealized)

b. as other comprehensive income or loss (unrealized)

a. As profit or loss

Under IFRS: If the financial assets are not intended to be kept until maturity, and the cash flows from these instruments are not predetermined and or do not occur on certain dates, consisting only of principal payments and interest, the instruments are classified as unrealized profit or loss in income statement.

Under US GAAP: All trading equity or debt securities are kept as unrealized gains or losses in the income statement.

b. As other comprehensive income or loss

Under IFRS: If the financial instruments are intended to collect income as well as intended to be sold before maturity. Also, if the company makes the irrevocable choice to measure the asset at the time of acquisition.

Under the US GAAP: Only debt instruments intended to sale before maturity can be categorized under other comprehensive income (or loss) and not equity.

4: Explain the financial reporting and disclosures related to non-current liabilities

Firms report their long-term debt in a single line in liabilities. The current portion of long term debt (interest payment and or the repayment of principle amount within one year) is reported in current liabilities. The details of long term debt are disclosed under footnotes and also in management's discussion and analysis. The footnotes are very helpful in determining the timing and amount of the payments. The footnotes normally consist following information.

Nature and Maturity of liability dates, Coated and effective interest/ market rates, Call and conversion options, Debt covenants, Assets which are pledged as security, the amount of debt maturing in each of the next five years.

The management's discussion and analysis cover the quantitative and qualitative aspects of debt like obligations due and future costs of capital respectively.

Deferred tax Liabilities disclosure: Following information is required to be disclosed relating to deferred tax items,

- Deferred tax assets and liabilities, valuation allowance and net change in valuation allowance over time.

- Unrecognized deferred tax liability (if any) for undistributed earnings.
- Effect of current year tax on temporary difference (and on DTA, DTL).
- Components of income tax expense.
- Reconciliation of reported income tax expense and the tax expense based.
- Tax losses carry forwards.

5: Calculate and interpret common-size balance sheets and related financial ratios

Divide the amount of each item on balance sheet by the amount of total assets and multiply result by 100. For example, if cash account is $10,000, divide $10,000 by total assets and then multiply by 100. [`(1000/total assets) x100`].

Do the same with other items like inventory, notes payable PP&E and bank loan etc.

Interpreting common size balance sheet:

First of all, we should look at the firm`s liquidity position. It means how their current assets are, compared to the current liabilities as a percentage of total assets. More percentage of current assets is, the better.

Secondly, we need to analyze the firm's **cash position** compared to current liabilities. Do we have enough cash to meet near term obligations if not then the company will have to pull in some cash from the sale of inventory (which is a bad sign).

Inventory: High levels of inventory percentage shows the company is potentially risking obsolescence and low level indicate the potential risk of stock shortage. Ideally these percentages must be close to industry norms or peer groups.

Now let's talk about the company's ability to meet long term obligations [long term liabilities/total assets]. What portion of total assets are financed or represented by long term debt. Higher level of long term debt as a proportion of total assets indicates that the company is not going to meet long term obligations and have risk of insolvency.

XYZ corp. LTD
Income statement
For the year ended 31Dec.2xx9 Vertical common size income statement

Sales	1000	(1000/1000)x10000=	100%
COGS	600	600/1000)x100 (600/1000)x100=	60%
GP	400	(400/1000)x100(400/1000)x100=	40%
Operating exp	40	(40/1000)x100=	4%
Admin exp	30	(30/1000)x100=	3%
Tax Expense	10	(10/1000)x100=	1%
Net profit	320	(320/1000)x100=	32%

XYZ corp. LTD
Balance sheet
As on 31Dec.2xx9

Year	2xx6	2xx7	2xx8	Horizontal common size balance sheet taking 2xx6 as base year		
Assets				2xx6 (%)	2xx7 (%)	2xx8 (%)
Cash and cash equivalents	100	120	140	(100/100)x100= 100%	(120/100)x100 = 120%	140
Account receivables	80	90	100	(80/80) x100 =100	(90/80)x100 =112.5	125
Inventory	200	210	220	100	105	110
PP&E	1000	1000	1000	100	100	100
Total assets	**1380**	**1420**	**1460**	**100**	**102.89**	**105.79**
Liabilities						
Account payables	100	105	110	100	105	110
Interest payable	50	55	60	100	110	120
long term debt	700	730	760	100	104.2857143	108.5714
total liabilities	**850**	**890**	**930**	**100**	**104.71**	**109.41**
common equity	530	530	530	100	100	100
Total liabilities & Equity	**1380**	**1420**	**1460**	**100**	**102.89%**	**105.79**

Learning Module 4
Analyzing Cash Flows Statement 1

1: Describe how the cash flow statement is linked to the income statement and the balance sheet

Link between cash flow statement and the balance sheet: Cash is an asset on the balance sheet reported at a specific date. Consecutive balance sheets tell us the cash balances at the beginning and the end of a period. Cash flow statement explains how the change occurred in between.

Relationship between cash flow, the balance sheet and the income statement: We need to look at individual asset or liability account separately. For example, if a company is selling goods we need to look how much of the cash is received and how much goes into receivables. By selling we get revenues which come into income statement. Receivables go into balance sheet while cash in the cash flow statement along with balance sheet.

Another relationship could be established between changing payables and cash flow statement, income statement and balance sheet. If the purchases are greater than the cash paid, we know that the payables will increase.

2: Describe the steps in the preparation of direct and indirect cash flow statements, including how cash flows can be computed using income statement and balance sheet data

Remember that regardless of the choice of direct or indirect CFI and CFF will be the same. Only CFO is affected by direct or indirect method.

Direct method: Under this method, net cash flows from operating activities are calculated by taking cash receipts from sales, adding interest and dividends received, and deducting cash payments for purchases, operating expenses, interest and income taxes.

<u>Cash collections:</u> From Account receivables, we take the opening receivables plus sale revenues minus closing balance of receivables and the resulting amount would be cash collected. In case of unearned revenues, add the opening balances of receivables and unearned revenue and add the closing balances of receivables and unearned revenue and proceed as normal.

<u>Cash payments:</u> We need to look at 1. Cash paid to suppliers and 2. Cash paid to employees.

Cash paid to suppliers is just like cash collections. Just look at how the payables accounts changes over the period and how much of that change is because of the purchase is bigger from the income statement.

Opening payables + purchases - ending balance of payables = cash paid out to suppliers.

If we are not given purchase figure but given inventory and cost of goods sold, we need to calculate purchases by following formula

(Ending inventory[1] - Beginning inventory[2]) + Cost of goods sold[3] = Inventory purchases

<u>Cash paid to employees:</u> Look for wages payable changes (balance sheet figure) and wages expense (in the income statement).

Opening balance of wages payable + wages expense (current) - ending balance = cash paid to employees.

<u>**O**perating expenses</u>: Start with the operating expenses from the income statement. We need to adjust from accrual base to cash base. Increase in prepayments shows use of cash. Increase in accrued liabilities indicates a source of cash. It means we have not paid so we have delayed the outflow.

<u>Cash paid for interest.</u>

---

1.   https://www.accountingtools.com/articles/2017/5/6/

ending-inventoryhttps:/www.accountingtools.com/articles/2017/5/6/ending-inventory

2.   https://www.accountingtools.com/articles/what-is-beginning-

inventory.htmlhttps:/www.accountingtools.com/articles/what-is-beginning-inventory.html

3.   https://www.accountingtools.com/articles/2017/5/4/cost-of-goods-sold

<u>Cash paid for tax</u>.

Remember depreciation is non-cash expense so we ignore it in direct method.

CFO by the indirect method:

1. Take the company's net income.
2. Remove any cash flow related to financing or investing activity because they are non-operating expenses. They will come under CFI and CFF.
3. Add any non-cash expense and minus any non-cash revenue.
4. Account for the sources and uses of cash as reflected in the changes to balance the accounts. When an asset increases it means we used cash so subtract the change. When an asset decreases the change is added. When a liability increases we delayed cash so add the change while a decrease in liability, means we used cash so subtract the change.
5. Any losses incurred in the sale of assets, any losses experienced in the sale of investments are added back because they are from investing activities. All the gains from these items must be subtracted.

1. Add all non-cash items like depreciation or amortization (of intangibles and bond discount).

Changes in the balance sheet

In this section we will see how operating assets and liabilities change from period to period.

Operating assets are receivables, inventory prepayments, deferred tax assets etc. Operating liabilities are payables, both trade payables and internal payables, accrued expenses and deferred tax liabilities.

Add back any decreases in operating assets or increases in operating liabilities because they are sources of cash. And subtract any increase in operating asset or decrease in operating liabilities because these are uses of cash.

Now have a look at CFI and CFF

Investing activities:

We need to figure out how much money was spent during the period on new asset. For that we need to look at the change in the asset account.

How much was the balance of the asset at the beginning of the period and how much was there at the end.

Ending balance of asset can be calculated as,

Beginning value of asset + money paid out for assets - money received in for assets sold = ending balance.

For each asset sold we need to consider both the book value of the asset and the gain or loss on the sale. If the sale gave us gain, we need to add that amount to the book value. A loss would have to be removed from the book value to get to the cash proceeds on the sale.

CFF financing activities: This includes transactions related to the company's capital structure. We need to look at the company's interactions with their creditors and their shareholders. With the creditors we may have inflows like the issuance of new debt. And outflows like repayment of existing debt. For the shareholders we have inflows from equity issuance and we have outflows for dividends and stock repurchase.

So, for creditors the net effect on cash flow could be represented like this.

New borrowings - any principal repaid. We are only looking at principal repaid because we are assuming that we have covered interest payments as part of CFO under IFRS.

For the shareholders we have equity issued inflows minus outflows for share repurchase and dividends paid.

3: demonstrate the conversion of cash flows from the indirect to direct method

CFI and CFF would be identical regardless of which method is chosen so we focus only on CFO.

Reason to convert from the indirect method to the direct method: CFO constructed by the direct method is a more valuable resource for an analyst than constructed by indirect method.

There are three steps of this conversion.

1. Disaggregate net income into total revenues and total expenses. And take totals of net revenues and total expenses separately (the income statement and balance sheet will be given).

We simply take the income statement for incomes and take a total and then separate out the expenses and take a total the net between those two figures should equal net income.

2. Disaggregated these two figures into their cash and non-cash components. Separate none cash revenues from revenues and separate none cash expenses from expenses.

3. Take the two cash components and built CFO using direct method from scratch. That means we're talking about cash collected from customers, cash paid to suppliers and employees operating expenses interest and tax.

4: Contrast cash flow statements prepared under International Financial Reporting Standards (IFRS) and US generally accepted accounting principles (US GAAP)

Under IFRS

Interest received and interest paid can be classified as either operating or financing activity. In terms of dividends IFRS offers us the choice between CFO and CFI.

Under US GAAP Interest and dividends received and interest paid are also classified as operating but dividends paid is not a component of CFO under U. S. GAAP.U. S. GAAP classifies dividends paid as a financing activity.

Another difference between these two is in form of income tax paid. Under US GAAP all taxes paid are reported as operating activities, even the tax is related to financing or investing activities. Under IFRS income tax is operating activity but if the tax is related to financing or investing activities, it is reported there (not in operating activities).

Learning Module 5
Analyzing Cash Flow Statements 2

1: analyze and interpret both reported and common-size cash flow statements

In this section we are going to understand company's cash flow situation.

Major sources and uses of cash: The uses and sources of cash of a firm is important part of cash flow analysis. When a firm is at start it most probably be generating negative cash flow from operations and this might be financed by external sources of cash like investing and or financing activities. After sometimes when the company is establishing itself it must generate positive cash flows from operating activities so it can return the external financing.

Operating cash flow:

First of all, we look at the trends in working capital. Cash flow statements constructed by indirect method show us how current assets (like inventory, receivables, payables, etc.) are changing over time and this will give us a great idea of how operating cash flows changing and why.

Interpretation: A positive operating cash flow is good if it is generated from operating activities. But positive cash flow is not good if it is being generated by selling current assets like inventory.

One important thing to note is that a cash flow figure higher (lower) than the net income indicates good (bad/ aggressive/ improper accounting) reporting quality.

Cash flow from investing activities: We need to consider each line item individually and find out what we have in uses of cash and sources of cash.

Uses of cash: Spending money on property plant and equipment or maybe we are acquiring companies for cash or investing in securities of other companies.

Sources of cash: Sources of cash in investing activities may be sale of property plant and equipment, selling of a business unit etc.

Interpretation: The important thing to note with sales is why the company is selling assets. Are they selling to invest in a better opportunity or they are generating cash to meet obligations?

Cash flow from financing activity:

This is also study of the uses and sources of cash.

Uses of cash: The Company may be repurchasing their own stock or paying dividends to equity shareholders.

Sources of cash: Sources of cash in CFI might be issuance of debt or equity issuance. An analyst must examine why the company has a positive or negative cash flow here.

Interpretation: An outflow means negative balance which might be a good thing if company is paying off debts but an inflow (positive balance) might be a bad thing if the company needs to generate cash from financing activities to pay dividends. If this is the case it means company`s CFO are not sufficient.

Common size analysis of the cash flow statement:

Just like the income statement and balance sheet, common size analysis of cash flow statement can also be useful in understanding the company's cash flow.

We have 2 methods for developing the common size cash flow statement.

1. The inflow/outflow method (revenue-based method). 2. The percentage sales method (as we did with income statement)

1. The inflow/outflow method (revenue-based method): we take each inflow as a percentage of the total inflow and each out flow as a percentage of the total outflow.

This method shows where the concentration of cash inflow/ outflow is. It is helpful to identify trends and future forecasting.

1. <u>The percentage sales method:</u> We simply take each line item as a percentage of sales revenue from the income statement. It is helpful to identify trends and future forecasting.

2: calculate and interpret free cash flow to the firm, free cash flow to equity, and performance and coverage cash flow ratios

Free cash flow (FCF): Free cash flow is the cash left after making capital expenditure (including growth). FCF is a measure of a company's financial performance, calculated as operating cash flow minus capital expenditures.

Two types of free cash flow. <u>1. Free cash flow to the firm</u> and <u>2. Free cash flow to equity.</u>

1. <u>**Free cash flow to the firm:** It is the cash available for both equity and debt holders. It means the cash available for dividends and interest payments after deduction of operating expenses and capital investment.</u>

We calculate FCFC from operating cash flow as follow

FCFF = Cash Flow from Operations[1] + Interest Expense[2] x (1 - Tax Rate[3]) – Capital expenditures. Remember that we need to add back in the interest expense (and eliminate the tax rate effect).

From net income we can calculate free cash by using following formula.

FCFF = net income[4] + non-cash charges[5] + interest x (1 - tax rate) - long-term investments[6] - investments in working capital

---

1.   http://www.investopedia.com/articles/investing/102413/cash-flow-statement-reviewing-cash-flow-operations.asp

2.   http://www.investopedia.com/terms/i/interestexpense.asp

3.   http://www.investopedia.com/terms/t/taxrate.asp

We take net income add back non-cash charges like depreciation and amortization again add back the after-tax interest expense and then we remove capital expenditure and working capital investment. The result would be same from both formulae.

<u>**Free cash flow to equity**</u>**: The** cash available just to the equity holders. It is the cash left after operating expenses fixed capital investment and borrowing costs. It shows how much cash is available to the equity shareholders of the company as dividends or stock buybacks, after all expenses, reinvestments, and debt repayments.

Calculation of FCFE: **FCFE= CFO -net capital expenditure + net borrowings**

Where Net borrowing = Debt issued – debt paid.

Cash flow ratios:

We are to discuss performance and coverage ratios.

Performance ratios:

Cash flow to revenue ratio: Formula; Cash flow to revenue ratio = CFO/ net revenues.

It tells us how much cash is generated per dollar of revenue.

Cash return on assets: Formula: CFO/ Average total assets. It tells us how much cash is generated per dollar of assets.

Cash return on equity: Formula: CFO/ Average shareholder`s equity. It tells us how much cash is generated per dollar of shareholders investment.

Cash flow to income ratio: Formula: CFO/ Operating income. It tells us the cash generating ability from operations.

Cash flow per share: Formula; (CFO – preferred dividend)/weighted average number of common shares.

Coverage ratios

---

4.   http://www.investopedia.com/terms/n/netincome.asp

5.   http://www.investopedia.com/terms/n/noncashcharge.asp

6.   http://www.investopedia.com/terms/l/longterminvestments.asp

Debt coverage ratio: Formula; CFO/ Total debt. It tells us about company's financial risk and leverage.

Interest coverage ratio: Formula; (CFO + tax paid + interest paid)/ interest paid. It measures the company's ability to pay interest. Sometimes under IFRS interest paid is given under financing activity. Just take that interest and nothing else needs to do.

Long term Debt repayment ratio: Formula; CFO/ cash paid on long term debt. It measures the company's ability to pay down debt obligations with operating cash flow.

Dividend payment ratio = CFO /dividends paid. It measures the company's ability to pay dividends out of operating cash.

Reinvestment ratio: formula; CFO/ Long term assets. It measures firm's ability to acquire long term assets by using CFO.

The investing and financing ratio: Formula; CFO/ Cash outflow for investing and financing activities. It tells us about the firm's ability to satisfy debts, pay dividends and asset purchase.

Learning Module 6
Analysis of Inventories

1: Describe the measurement of inventory at the lower of cost and net realisable value and its implications for financial statements and ratios

In this section we are to look at the measurement of inventory value under IFRS and U. S. GAAP

***Under IFRS** we must value inventory at the lower of cost or net realizable value.*

Net realizable value = expected sales price - completion costs - selling costs.

If cost is lower than net realizable value then it must be recorded at cost. And if subsequently net realizable value falls below cost the value of inventory must then be written down to account for that loss in value. And that loss would have to be reflected on the income statement.

After written down if realizable value subsequently increases again. IFRS allows us to reverse the original right down that took us from the original cost level down to the lower net realizable value level. So, we post an increase to the inventory account and the gain to the income statement. It is known as a reversal of a right down.

These transactions would generally occur in a contra account called a valuation allowance account so that changes in value are kept separate from initial cost.

Under US GAAP inventory is valued at the lower of cost or market.

Market value = replacement cost, (but cannot be greater than Net realizable value). Or

Market value < NRV - normal profit margin.

If replacement cost >NRV, then market is net realizable value. If replacement cost is, NRV - normal profit margin, then market is NRV -normal profit margin.

Again, in this case where current market value was below the reported valuation of inventory a write down is performed and a loss is recognized on the income statement.

But U. S. GAAP does not allow write ups or reversals in the case of a subsequent increase in value.

One interesting point to note: because firms reporting inventory levels based on the LIFO method will have their inventory value based on older and likely lower cost levels. They will be less likely to experience a right down.

When we write down inventory to net realizable value it affects financial statements in many ways as follows

- Inventory is included in current assets, a written in inventory will decrease in current assets and also in total assets.
- A decrease in total assets causes increase in total asset turnover (**Sales / Average Total Assets) and debt to assets ratio.**
- Inventory turnover (COGS/ Average inventory) increases but days inventory in hand and cash conversion cycle decreases.
- Shareholder's equity decreased so the debt to equity ratio increases.
- Due to increase in COGS gross profit margin, operating profit margin and net profit margin decreases.
- Percentage decrease in net income is often more than percentage decrease in assets and or equity. So, return on assets and return on equity decreases.
- The current ratio (current assets/ current liabilities) decreases. Not effect on quick ratio as we do not include inventory in it.
- In subsequent years of written down COGS may be decrease as we have lower inventory value so the profit margins will

increase and so the ROA and ROE.

2: Calculate and explain how inflation and deflation of inventory costs affect the financial statements and ratios of companies that use different inventory valuation methods

When prices are rising (inflation) LIFO will give us higher cost of goods sold and lower value of inventory in hand. It's because most recent units are sold first which are costly than older units. It means less gross profit and net profit will be reported in income statement.

With increasing prices FIFO will give us lower cost of goods sold but higher inventory in hand. This is because of the older units with cheaper prices are sold first while the newer units (with higher prices) will be kept in stock. It means we would be having higher gross and net profits than LIFO method.

When prices are falling (deflation) the pattern will be other way around. In this situation LIFO gives us less cost of goods sold and higher inventory in hand while higher gross and net profits.

FIFO will give us higher COGS, lower inventory in hand, lower gross and net profits.

Also, with rising prices LIFO gives us lower tax expense as COGS would be higher.

3: Describe the presentation and disclosures relating to inventories and explain issues that analysts should consider when examining a company's inventory disclosures and other sources of information

Disclosures related to inventory

Under IFRS and US GAAP companies are required to disclose the following

- Accounting policies followed related to measurement. (It means the valuation method and cost flow formula).
- Carrying value by classification. (That means a breakdown of inventory value split out into raw materials, production

supplies, works in progress and finished units ready for sale).
- The value of units held at fair value less selling costs.
- The cost of goods sold or cost of sales.
- Any write downs recognize in the period.
- Any reversals of write downs recognize in the period.
- The circumstances leading to write downs or reversals (GAAP does not allow reversal).
- Any inventory pledged as collateral against liabilities.

Changes in inventory

A firm can change inventory cost flow methods normally retrospectively (the previous year's financial statements are restated using new cost flow method). There is an exception to this rule when a firm changes its inventory method to LIFO. In this case, the change is applied prospectively. It means changes in previous periods are not required for re-adjustments.

Under IFRS, the firm must explain that the change will provide reliable and more relevant information. Under U.S. GAAP, the firm must explain why the change in inventory method is preferable.

Issues that analysts should consider when examining a company's inventory disclosures and other sources of information

Some firms, like wholesaler and retailers (also called merchandising firms), do not manufacture goods. They only buy and sell. Their goods are ready to sale. So, they record inventory in one account only in the balance sheet.

Other firms who manufacture goods record goods in usually three accounts, raw material, work in process and finished goods.

An analyst must use this information about inventory along with management discussion and analysis, industry reports and other data to determine about future revenues of the firm.

Let's say a firm has more inventories in hand. It can be related to increase in demand so the firm is collecting more inventories. If sales are reduced with an increase in inventory and finished goods. It can be described as reduction in demand and inventory can be getting obsolete and there is a risk of inventory write down.

Higher inventory turnover is good but if it is combined with low sales growth, it means firm is not holding adequate inventory which can cause a further reduction in sales.

High inventory turnover may also mean that an inventory write-down has occurred which is a sign of poor inventory management. But higher sale growth with higher inventory turnover may reflect efficiency.

Learning Module 7
Analysis of Long-Term Assets

1: Compare the financial reporting of the following types of intangible assets: purchased, internally developed, and acquired in a business combination

Intangible assets are assets that do not bear a physical substance.

They are of two types. Identifiable assets and un-identifiable assets.

Identifiable intangible: These are assets that represent a contractual or legal right that can be separated from the owning entity under expected to generate a future economic benefit.

These assets might include.

- Patents.
- Copyrights.
- Brand recognition or a trademark.

An unidentifiable intangible asset an asset that bears no physical substance and it does not match the criteria of identifiable intangible assets.

One good example of unidentifiable intangible asset is <u>good will</u>, the excessive purchase price over the fair value of assets acquired.

There are two other broad categories of intangible asset.

- Assets with finite lives
- Assets with indefinite life

Asset with a finite life must be amortized (Similar to a tangible asset). Whereas the cost of an asset with an indefinite life will not be amortized but will be tested annually for impairment.

If impairment occurs then the assets value will be written down on the balance sheet and the firm report a loss on their income statement.

Accounting for intangibles depends on how they were acquired.

- Assets might be purchased.
- Developed internally.
- Or acquired as part of the business combination.

When an asset is purchased, the accounting treatment is quite similar to tangible long lived assets.

The purchase price is assumed to be equal to fair value and that's the figure used to record the asset on the balance sheet. Then

For assets that were developed internally the accounting treatment is a bit different.

When an asset is purchased the company will have one easily identifiable transaction that can drive an asset being capitalized on the balance sheet.

Assets which are developed internally will have come about through a series of expenses the company would have recognized in the periods which they were incurred. The company will have spent money over time on a wide variety of expenses and it's the combination of all of these varying expenses that lead the company to own this intangible asset. So, the company will recognize a series of expenditures on their income statement over time. These together will develop into an intangible asset that they own.

A good example would be continuous expenditures on R & D program or an advertising or marketing plan.

Over time these might develop into a recognizable brand and brand recognition.

The differing accounting treatments we have seen here will spark a major difference between the financial statements of companies who purchase assets and those who have developed them internally.

On the one hand you have companies with assets on the balance sheet compared to companies that do not have assets to report. This is because companies who develop their assets internally have expensed their acquisition costs as they were being developed.

At the same time, you have these purchasing companies recognizing expenditures as investing cash flows. While the companies developing the assets are recognizing these expenses as operating cash flows.

Intangibles acquired as part of the business combination: Assets acquired through a business combination are accounted for using the acquisition methods. Assets acquired are recorded on the balance sheet of the acquirer at fair value. The difference between the overall purchase price and the combined amount attributable to the acquired assets is recorded as good will.

It's important to know that this is what we consider good will to be an on identifiable intangible asset. It cannot be separated from the acquired business.

2: Explain and evaluate how impairment and derecognition of property, plant, and equipment, and intangible assets affect the financial statements and ratios

Impairment: Impairment reduces the value of asset (tangible and intangible). We record it as loss in income statement; reduce it from retained earnings (equity) and asset. So, the Return on assets (ROA) and Return on equity (ROE) ratios are lower as net income declined. In coming years, as we have impaired the asset's value, the depreciation expense will be less. So, the net income would be higher (than that if the asset was not impaired) so does the ROA and ROE. Asset turnover ratio would be higher in impairment year and subsequent years as asset's value is lower now. As the impairment is a non-cash loss, there would be no effect on cash flow statement.

Analysis of impairment: when company impairs its assets, that means the management failed to depreciate or amortize the asset according to the market conditions. It also means that they were recognizing less expense and more income in previous years. Recognition of impairment can be a good opportunity for management to manipulate earnings and ROE, ROA etc. sometimes management decides not to recognize the impairment loss until the year of good earnings to show smooth income pattern. On the other hand, early impairment loss could be done by management to show higher income and ROE, ROA in coming years. A good level of judgment from analyst is required to understand the reason behind the impairment.

De-recognition of Assets: De-recognition is the process by which a company removes an asset from its financial statements.

There are three situations whereby an asset will be de recognized.

◈ When the asset is sold.
◈ Exchanged.
◈ Or abandoned.

When an asset is sold the difference between the sale proceeds in the assets carrying value will go into income statement either as a gain or as a loss. That same figure will also need to be recognized on the cash flow statement as an investing cash inflow.

If an old asset is exchanged for a newer one we will be removing the carrying value of the old asset from the balance sheet and adding the fair value of the new asset as well as that a gain or loss will hit the income statement to reflect the difference between the fair value of the new asset and the carrying value of the old asset.

If an asset is abandoned or retired: The treatment is very similar to a sale only in this case there will be no sale proceeds. There will be a loss to the income statement and since no cash changes hands the cash flow statement will not be affected.

3: Analyze and interpret financial statement disclosures regarding property, plant, and equipment and intangible assets

Financial statement disclosures regarding property plant and equipment are helpful for an analyst to understand company's fixed assets and choice of depreciation and or amortization taken. One most common metric used by analyst form this information is to calculate average age of an asset. Average age calculation has two benefits:

⬦ The average useful life gives us the timings of future capital expenditure and financing requirement of the firm.

⬦ To estimate if the older asset might be giving the owning entity a comparative disadvantage.

Following are some useful calculations for analyst:

Average age of assets in years = (Accumulated depreciation)/(current year depreciation expense) , this calculation s more accurate in firms using straight line depreciation method. The answer is highly dependent on the types of assets used.

Total useful life of asset in years = (Historical cost)/(annual depreciation expense), we know that historical cost is the cost of asset before deduction of any depreciation.

Remaining useful life (in years) = (Ending net balance of PP&E)/(Annual depriciation), we know ending net PP&E = Gross PP&E – Accumulated depreciation

The remaining useful life can also be calculated as, average depreciable life - average age

Annual capital expenditures to depreciation expense ratio: another common measure used by analysts to determine whether the firm is replacing its PP&E at the same rate as its assets are being depreciated.

Learning Module 8
Topics in Long-Term Liabilities and Equity

1: Explain the financial reporting of leases from the perspectives of the lessors and lessees

Lessee`s perspective:

Under IFRS the lease can be classified as either operating or finance lease. The choice of classification depends upon the economic substance of the transaction. For a lease to be considered as Finance lease (under IFRS) any of the following criteria must met

- At the end of lease title of the asset is to be transferred to lessee,
- The lessee can purchase the asset in future at significantly lower price than its fair value.
- The asset is specialized made for lessee (only the lessee can use the asset without any significant modification)
- The lease agreement covers major portion of the useful life of asset.
- The present value of payments of leased asset is significantly equal to the fair value of that asset.

US GAAP also describe some rules to classify a lease as a finance (in US GAAP Finance lease is called capital) lease. The US GAAP rules are same as IFRS but considered more specific than IFRS. For US GAAP any of the following criteria must meet for finance lease;

- At the end of lease, title of the asset is to be transferred to lessee,
- The lessee can purchase the asset in future at significantly

lower price than its fair value.

- A *bargain purchase option* permits the lessee to purchase the asset in future at significantly lower price than its market fair value.
- The lease agreement covers 70% or more useful life of asset.
- The present value of payments of leased asset is 90% or more to the fair value of that asset.

If none of the above criteria is met the lease is considered as operating lease. A lessee prefers operating lease in general as no asset or liability is reported in it. With finance lease lessee reports asset and liability.

Lease to be reported by lessee:

Operating lease: No entry is made at the inception of the lease (but as discussed above the future obligations must be disclosed under footnotes). Only rental income equal to lease payment is recorded in income statement as expense. In cash flow statement lease payment is recorded as cash outflow under operating activities.

Finance lease: A lower of present value of future minimum lease payments (cash outflows) or the fair value is recorded as liability and asset in balance sheet. That asset is depreciated annually. As the time goes the depreciation and interest payments are recorded as expense in income statement. Interest on lease can be calculated as,

Lease payments as beginning of period x interest rate.

In terms of cash flow statement, the total lease payment is separated as principal and interest payment. When using IFRS the principal amount goes into investing activities while interest payment can go in either financing or operating activities. Under US GAAP interest amount goes into operating activities while principal amount goes into financing activities (as outflows).

Impact of financing vs operating lease on lessee`s financial statements

	Finance lease	Operating lease
Assets	Higher	Lower
Total liabilities	Higher	Lower
Net income (at inception of lease)	Lower	Higher
Net income (in subsequent years)	Higher	Lower
EBIT	Higher	Lower
Over all net income (in all periods)	Same	Same
Operating cash flow	Higher	Lower
Cash flow from financing	Lower	Higher
Total cash flow	Same	Same

Impact of financing vs operating lease on lessee`s ratios

	Finance lease	**Operating lease**
Current ratio (CA/CL)	Lower	Higher
Working capital (CA – CL)	Lower	Higher
Asset turnover (Revenue / TA)	Lower	Higher
Return on assets (in early periods) (NI / TA)	Lower	Higher
Return on equity (in early periods) (NI / SE)	Lower	Higher
Debt / Assets	Higher	Lower
Debt / Equity	Higher	Lower

In finance lease all ratios are worse. In financial statements we see some benefits like EBIT is higher (because interest is not subtracted in

EBIT calculation), CFO is higher (because principal repayments goes into CFF) and higher net income in subsequent years in finance lease.

Lessor`s perspective

Under IFRS the criteria for operating or finance lease is same for lessor. However, US GAAP is a little bit different here. Under U.S. GAAP, if any of the criteria of finance lease is met plus the collection of lease payments are reasonably certain then it is finance lease otherwise is treated as operating lease.

We know that with operating lease, the lessor reports rental income and depreciate the leased asset. With capital lease, the lessor removes the asset (from balance sheet) and creates a lease investment account as lease receivable.

Reporting by the Lessor

From the perspective of lessor, a lease is also classified into one of two categories, 1. Finance lease 2. Operating lease.

Finance lease: when the lease is treated as finance lease the lessor remove the asset from the balance sheet. If the lessor is manufacturer of that asset then the will recognize present value of lease payments as sale price and cost of the asset as carrying value. So, the difference between sale price and cost of asset is gross profit (as normal sale of asset).

If the lessor is not manufacturer or dealer but only providing lease then the gross profit at inception of lease is zero. It means the sale price is recognized as present value of lease payments. As at the inception of lease the asset is removed from balance sheet and an equal amount of lease receivable (equal to the present value of lease payments) is created. As the lease goes on the principal amount of lease received reduces the lease receivable (as the lessor is selling the asset at fair market value and loaned the amount to lessee). The other part of lease received (other than principal) is interest and it is recognized as interest income. In cash flow statement interest received goes into CFO and the principal (lease) reduction goes into CFI as inflow.

Operating lease: In operating lease the lessor treats it as rental income. The lessor keeps the asset in balance sheet and depreciates it.

2: Explain the financial reporting of defined contribution, defined benefit, and stock-based compensation plans

Pension: It is the amount of funds collected from employees during their services. These funds are used to support the person after retirement.

The two broad categories of pension plan are defined contribution plan and defined pension plan.

Defined contribution plan: It is a retirement plan in which employer contributes a certain amount of money in each period (i.e. monthly) into employee's retirement account. The contribution may depend on employee's contribution, employee's experience, duration of employee's services etc. The employee can also contribute same or different amount. The firm provides no promises about the future value of the plan. The money is invested and it can earn positive or negative earnings. The investment decisions are left to empl0yee. The employee bears all the risks involved linked to investment.

Financial reporting requirement: Financial reporting requirements for defined contribution plan are straight forward. Amount contributed by employer is his pension expense and there is no future liability to report on balance sheet.

Defined benefit plan: It is a retirement plan in which the employer assumes risk of future value of the plan. The employer promises to pay certain periodic payments to employee in future (after retirement). In this plan the employer contributes certain amount (the employee may or may not contribute) into fund and generally sends the amount to an institution which is specialized for investment. The employer makes sure a certain future value of the fund. The retirement benefits usually depend on employee's years of service, or the compensations at retirement. For example, an employee who is to be entitled 3% of her salary (0f $200000) and served for 30 years may get

200000 x 30 x 2% = $120000

Financial reporting requirement: Financial reporting is complicated here. The employer needs to estimate value of future obligation of defined benefit plan. The variables used to forecast are mortality rate, future compensation amount (salary), retirement age and discount rate.

If the fair value of plan asset is greater than future obligation then plan is called <u>overfunded</u> plan and <u>an asset named net pension</u> is to be recorded into balance sheet of employer. On the other hand, if fair value is less than pension obligation the plan is called <u>underfunded</u> and the employer has to record <u>net pension liability</u> in balance sheet.

Reporting under IFRS

1. Service cost/past service cost + Interest income/ expense go into Income statement (under pension expense)

3. Re-measurement +Actuarial gains/losses + Actual return + Expected return go into Balance sheet (under shareholder`s equity)

Reporting under US GAAP

1. Service cost/past service cost + Interest income/ expense go into Income statement (under pension expense).

2. Expected return on assets +Actuarial gains/losses go into Balance sheet (under shareholder`s equity) (the amortization of expected return on assets +Actuarial gains/losses goes back into income statement as expense.

First, we need to define these terms;

Service cost: It is the present value of the retirement benefits which employee is entitled to take in current year.

Past service costs: It is the changes in the value of defined benefit plan in previous periods. Interest expense or interest income is equal to the value of asset in the beginning of the year x interest rate.

The interest rate depends on the management`s judgment but it should reflect the yield rate of A rated bond.

Actuarial gains and losses are the difference between the actual pension payments and the expected amount. Actuarial gain = amount paid < expected. Actuarial loss = amount paid > expected.

Under IFRS

Any change in net liability or asset is calculated and annually calculated and reported in financial statements. These changes are recorded in other comprehensive income, in net income or in balance sheet. Under IFRS service cost, interest expense, expected return on plan assets goes into income statement, and then goes to balance sheet ultimately. On the other hand, past services cost, actuarial gains or losses goes into balance sheet.

Under US GAAP

Under US GAAP there are five parts of net pension asset or liability. Service costs, net interest expense, and the expected return are the net pension expense goes into income statement.

Past service costs and actuarial gains or losses goes into other comprehensive income. These two are amortized into current pension expense annually. It means the firm can report their pension expense and net pension obligation over the term of the life of plan.

For a manufacturing firm the IFRS and US GAAP pension expense is allocated to cost of goods sold and inventory (for direct labor) and to administrative expenses and salaries (for administrative services). Therefore, pension expense does not show in income statement. Footnotes must be examined carefully to understand the pension expense.

Stocked base compensation plan

This plan ensures that employees are motivated to work towards the same goals as shareholders. Employees are compensated with equity shares instead of other types of payment. This type of plan is frequently utilized in senior management. Companies are obligated to disclose this type of plan in their financial statement. The recognition of fair value of compensation occurs at the payment date, resulting in an expense. Any subsequent changes in the value of shares do not impact the financial statements. Stock grants and stock options are two popular types of shared-based compensation plans.

3: Describe the financial statement presentation of and disclosures relating to long-term liabilities and share-based compensation

Firms report their long-term debt in a single line in liabilities. The current portion of long term debt (interest payment and or the repayment of principle amount within one year) is reported in current liabilities. The details of long term debt are disclosed under footnotes and also in management's discussion and analysis. The footnotes are very helpful in determining the timing and amount of the payments. The footnotes normally consist following information.

Nature and Maturity of liability dates, Coated and effective interest/ market rates, Call and conversion options, Debt covenants, Assets which are pledged as security, the amount of debt maturing in each of the next five years.

The management`s discussion and analysis cover the quantitative and qualitative aspects of debt like obligations due and future costs of capital respectively.

Disclosures related to compensation plans are discussed in previous Los.

Learning Module 9
Analysis of Income Taxes

1: Contrast accounting profit, taxable income, taxes payable, and income tax expense and temporary versus permanent differences between accounting profit and taxable income

Most of the times income tax rules are different than financial statement rules. So, the income tax payable (in the perspective of income tax authorities) is may be different than recognized in income statement.

Some most common terminologies of income tax

Taxable income: *It is* the base income on which *income* tax authorities imposes tax. It is the income on which the tax is deductible by law.

Taxes payable: it is the liability arises from taxable income. It is the current tax expense calculated from taxable income according the tax laws.

Income tax paid: It is the actual outflow from income as tax expense.

Tax loss carried forward: it is the current or past losses that can be used to reduce taxable income (and current tax payable) in future. It causes deferred tax liability.

<u>Tax base:</u> Amount of an asset or liability used for tax calculation and reporting purpose.

Financial reporting terminologies related to income tax:

Accounting profit: It is also called income before tax or earnings before tax. This is pre-tax income calculated according to the financial accounting standards.

Income tax expense: Income tax expense = taxes payable + changes in deferred tax liabilities – changes in deferred tax asset. It is the income tax recognized in financial statements (income tax and any changes in deferred tax liabilities and assets).

Deferred tax liabilities: This is a balance sheet item. It shows any excess of income tax expense over income taxes payable. It is expected to be paid in future. A very good example for this is when a company chose to use accelerated depreciation for tax purpose but uses straight line method for financial reporting. Using accelerated depreciation method, the depreciation expense will be higher in first periods and the tax payable would be less. Off course the tax payable would be higher in later periods. For this company choose to recognize higher tax payable in first periods so the affect will be offset in coming years.

Deferred tax assets: This is a balance sheet item. It shows any excess of income tax payable over income taxes expense. It is expected to be recovered in future. When this happens, we carry forward tax loss.

Valuation allowance: When deferred tax asset is not likely to be realized we reduce the asset. That reduction is called valuation allowance.

Carrying value: Net balance sheet value of an asset or liability.

Permanent difference: A difference between taxable income (tax return) and pretax income unlikely to reverse in the future.

Temporary difference: This is a difference between the tax base of an asset/liability and the carrying value of an asset/liability that will result in either higher or lower tax amount of tax in current period. This difference would offset in future that's why it is called temporary difference. The examples of this will come after a little bit in this section.

2: Explain how deferred tax liabilities and assets are created and the factors that determine how a company's deferred tax liabilities and assets should be treated for the purposes of financial analysis

Normally the treatment of accounting items is different for tax reporting and financial reporting. This difference is due to following reasons

- The timing of revenue recognition is different for financial reporting than tax purposes.
- Some gains and or losses have difference in recognition for both.
- Some revenues are to be recognized in financial statements but cannot be recognized for tax returns, and vice versa.
- Some assets ad or liabilities have different carrying value for tax and financial reporting purposes.
- Some financial statement adjustments may not be recognized or adjusted in tax base of those items.
- Some tax losses from past can reduce future tax return.

Deferred tax liability: When income tax expense is greater than taxes payable due to temporary differences the deferred tax liability is created (it has to be paid in future). It can be caused by following reasons:

- Revenues and or gains are recognized in the income statement but not yet included on the tax return due to temporary differences.
- Expenses and or losses are used to tax deduction but not are recognized in the income statement.

A most common cause of deferred tax liability is when an accelerated depreciation method is used on the tax purposes but straight-line depreciation method is used in the income statement.

Deferred Tax Assets: When taxes payable are greater than income tax expense (in income statement) due to temporary differences a deferred tax asset is created. Following reason can cause deferred tax asset creation:

- Revenues and or gains are not yet recognized in the income Statement but used for tax purposes.
- Expenses and or losses are recognized in the income statement but not yet used for tax deduction.
- Carried forward losses reduce future taxable income.

Tax loss carry forwards are used to reduce future taxable income.

Treatment for Analytical Purposes

If deferred tax liabilities are to reverse in the future, they should be treated as liabilities (for analysis). If not, they must be classified as equity

The analyst has to decide when and why we should treat them as liability or equity on case by case basis.

3: Calculate, interpret, and contrast an issuer's effective tax rate, statutory tax rate, and cash tax rate

4: Analyze disclosures relating to deferred tax items and the effective tax rate reconciliation and explain how information included in these disclosures affects a company's financial statements and financial ratios

Statutory tax rate: It is the tax rate of jurisdiction where firm operates.

Effective tax rate: It is derived from the formula,

$$\text{Effective tax rate} = \frac{\text{income tax expense}}{\text{pre tax accountin income}}$$

Cash tax rate: Rate of tax paid in cash.

Disclosure: Following information is required to be disclosed relating to deferred tax items,

- Deferred tax assets and liabilities, valuation allowance and

net change in valuation allowance over time.
- Unrecognized deferred tax liability (if any) for undistributed earnings.
- Effect of current year tax on temporary difference (and on DTA, DTL).
- Components of income tax expense.
- Reconciliation of reported income tax expense and the tax expense based.
- Tax losses carry forwards.

Analysis of effective tax rate reconciliation

Sometimes reported income tax expense is different from the amount based on statutory income tax rate. We know that statutory tax rate is the tax rate that is imposed by law in that area. Following could be the reasons of those differences.

- Difference in tax rate in different jurisdictions.
- Permanent tax differences like tax exemptions, tax credits, none deductible expenses, and difference between operating income and capital gains.
- Changes in tax laws of the jurisdictions in which firm or its subsidiary operate.
- Deferred tax assets arise from reinvestment of earnings of foreign and domestic affiliates.
- Tax holidays

An analyst has to understand each of these reconciliation items, their impact on future earnings, its past changes and expected future changes in these elements.

It's also important for analyst to include only those items in her analysis which are continuous in nature. For example, different tax rates in different states (or countries) income exempted from tax, tax credits, none deductible expenses are continuous in nature. While tax holidays and capital gain taxes are periodic. The footnotes and MD &A should be reviewed to understand the nature of an item.

Learning Module 10
Financial Reporting Quality

1: Compare financial reporting quality with quality of reported results (including quality of earnings, cash flow, and balance sheet items)

Financial reporting quality: Financial reporting quality is the usefulness of a financial document / set of financial documents for those who need to make decisions about the firm. Generally, users of financial documents are investors, creditors, potential business partners etc.

Financial documents are useful if they fulfill following conditions

- Relevance
- Timeliness
- Faithful representation.

Relevance means the information generated by financial documents must impact the decision making of users of these documents. Relevance also means the information must be material.

Timeliness means the information must be provided in time when the users need to make decisions about the company.

Faithful representation means completeness, neutrality, and the absence of errors.

Quality of reported results: It means sustainability and level of earnings. How sustainable the business is to produce this level of earnings. Higher earnings due to the events which are not likely to occur (like changes in exchange rate) in future does not means a sustainable level of earnings. On the other hand, attaining efficiency and reduction in cost may lead to sustainability. A higher level of earnings means that earnings are high enough to fulfill operational needs as well as a decent return to investor.

A higher quality of financial reporting may not guarantee a higher quality of reported results. Higher quality means the financial documents are GAAP compliance but may not be sustainable.

2: Describe a spectrum for assessing financial reporting quality

The spectrum is the bedrock upon which the quality of financial reporting is evaluated. On one end of the spectrum are reports that are of low quality and unreliable, while on the other end are reports that have excellent quality and sustained earnings.

GAAP, Decision-useful, Sustainable earnings: These financial reports are of exceptional quality, following GAAP guidelines, offering valuable insights, and accurately reflecting long-term earnings (earnings reported are from activities which were expected to continue into the future). These reports possess the characteristics of being relevant, accurately representing the information, allowing for comparison, being verifiable, providing timely information, and being easily understandable. Strong earnings contribute to the company's valuation.

GAAP, Decision-Useful, but Sustainable?: At the second level of the spectrum, there are reports that follow GAAP and provide valuable information for decision making. However, these reports may reflect earnings that are not sustainable in the long term. It indicates that the earnings have lower quality despite the high quality of reporting. There could be various economic and industry factors that have led to a decline in long-term earnings.

Within GAAP, but Biased Choices: The next level adheres to GAAP guidelines, but may involve subjective decision-making. When the financial reports adhere to the GAAP, but the accounting and measurement choices do not accurately reflect the information. This impedes the ability to analyze the company's performance. Companies often make biased choices when presenting their reports, using tactics like aggressive accounting, conservative choices, and earning smoothing. These strategies can distort the true picture of their financial situation.

Within GAAP, but Earnings Management: The next level is within GAAP but earning management. In this type of reporting, the management intentionally makes biased choices to distort the accurate picture. Biased choices are usually unintentional, while earnings management means intentional efforts to manipulate earnings and the financial position of the company. Postponing the research and development expenditures and showing them to the next accounting period, increasing the current earnings, is one example of intentional earning management. Accounting decisions regarding bad debts or the impairment of assets are also part of earning management. User can conclude inaccurate future estimates. Biases can be aggressive (inflated results), conservative, or smoothening (to show smooth results by reducing earnings in better situations to offset bad earnings in other periods, being conservative in years of good performance, and being aggressive in years of poor performance).

Non-Compliant Accounting: In this level, accounting that does not adhere to GAAP is indicative of unreliable financial reporting. These reports may be partially fictitious information but does not obey the generally accepted accounting standards. These reports may overstate or understate some items improper calculations and estimates of assets and liabilities. It is difficult to assess the firm and much more difficult to compare it to competitors with this kind of information.

Fictitious Transactions: This is the bottom of the quality of the spectrum of financial reporting. In this case, financial reports show fictitious events and transactions to fraud the investors. These are the entries which did not occur in reality but have been added intentionally.

3: Explain the difference between conservative and aggressive accounting

The unbiased and neutral financial documents are more valuable in the views of an analyst (and for other users). It means management neither uses conservative accounting nor aggressive accounting.

Conservative accounting: In conservative accounting the management tend to decrease the firm`s current earnings and financial position so reports less income and weak financial position. Use of conservatism the tendency of future earnings increases.

Aggressive accounting: If management decides to increase current earnings and financial position it is called aggressive accounting. In this method the future earnings tend to decrease.

Both aggressive and conservative accounting is not desirable. Both of these are biased and used by management to smooth their earnings (and reduce volatility) over several years.

Following are some examples of conservative vs aggressive accounting (based on management`s choices and estimates)

Aggressive	*Conservative*
Capitalizing cost (so the earnings would be higher)	Expensing costs (so the earning would be lower)
More useful life of assets (less depreciation expense, higher net income)	Less useful life of assets (higher depreciation less net income)
Higher salvage value (less depreciation)	Lower estimates of salvage value (more depreciation)
Declining balance or straight-line depreciation	Double accelerating depreciation method
Higher accruals of receivables (less bad debts)	Less receivable estimates (more bad debts)
Late impairment recognition	Early recognition of impairment

**4: Describe motivations that might cause management to issue financial reports that are not high quality and conditions that are

conducive to issuing low-quality, or even fraudulent, financial reports

There are three things which led management to produce low quality or even fraudulent reports,

Opportunity

Motivation

Rationalization

1. **Opportunity:** When management is given opportunity, they might take it. It mostly happens when internal controls are weak, the board is ineffective or a lack of fear about the punishment.

2. **Motivations:** There are many motivations for management to produce low quality reports. For example, when manager is trying to maintain business competitiveness by hiding a period of poor performance.

Earnings have been the most important measure in the eyes of management in terms of setting targets. Beating prior years or analyst`s expectations is a very common goal.

Sometime the motivation is to avoid a penalty from a debt covenants perspective.

3. **Rationalization:** By rationalization we mean that a person is interested in justifying their fraudulent or bias decisions.

The management seeks opportunities to justify or defend their actions. So, they believe that their choices are either in their own self-interest or in the interests of those they intend to support.

5: Describe mechanisms that discipline financial reporting quality and the potential limitations of those mechanisms

There are four mechanisms that contribute to the level of quality of a company's financial reports.

- Market forces and investor expectations.
- Regulatory authorities.
- Auditors

- Private contracting.

Market forces and investor expectations: We know that a company's cost of capital depends on the business risks and investor's expectation of the risk. When a company produces low quality reports, expectation of risk is increased and investors will demand higher rate of return in order to invest or lend in than company. So, the cost of capital increases. On the other hand by persistently producing higher quality reports the cost of capital would be reduced.

Sometimes here, a conflict of interest arises. Management wants to reduce cost of capital but they might have an incentive for which they have to produce low quality reports.

Regulatory authorities: There are several authorities around the globe to establish and enforce rules and standards to protect market participants. **For example,** in Europe the European securities and markets authority, FCA the financial conduct authority in UK and SEC, the Securities and Exchange Commission in USA.

Along these there are many regional regulators and members of the IOSCO, the international organization of securities commissions, the global standard setter for the security sector.

These authorities have number of ways to influence and implement higher quality in financial reporting. For example,

Registration requirements: This means that companies have become transparent before offering securities. These regulatory authorities are a first step check on the company.

Disclosure requirements: These are several documents and their contents which a company is required to submit. Regulatory authorities have rules for these submissions and disclosures regarding those submissions.

Auditing regulators: These regulators ask the company to obtain unqualified reports of independent auditors to ensure best accounting practices.

Enforcement power of regular: Regulatory authorities have power to fine, power to suspend for any wrong doing of the companies.

A limitation is to be discussed here. If a regulator is not strong enough he may not be able to ensure high quality reports to the users.

Auditors: This is the simplest of four mechanisms. When an independent auditor cleared the financial documents, the users get some assurance that the proper methods of estimates, disclosures and related accounting standards have been followed.

Regrettably, the work of auditor is limited. It is limited to the information provided to the auditor. If management deliberately mislead the auditor the auditor`s report might also be misleading.

Mostly auditor`s opinion is based on a sample of accounts. If the fraud is hided in depth, it might be hard for auditor to detect.

The auditors do not seek out fraudulent activity intentionally. They use designated set of processes to check if the reports are accounting standard compliant and fair.

Private contracting: Private contracting parties is another important source for financial discipline. For example, a lending party would calculate different financial measures and come up with better interpretations. Parties who do business with a particular company have an incentive to look closely in their business affairs.

A limitation here, when there is penalty from lenders, for certain events like lower earnings the borrower has some incentive to produce low quality reports.

6: Describe presentation choices, including non-GAAP measures, that could be used to influence an analyst's opinion

Accounting choices (in calculation and presentation of financial data) made in financial reporting must be understood by analyst in order to evaluate company`s financial reports. These choices affect usefulness of reports.

Sometimes firms use some measures not defined in GAAP or not required in GAAP to look financial reports better. Normally these are excluded from financial reports. Justifications given by management for this exclusion include

- These items are of non-recurring
- They are non-cash items
- By excluding these items, they are improving comparability.

In US the firms which uses non-GAAP measures are required to disclose following

Show the most comparable GAAP measure with same prominence

Give justification why non-GAAP measure is useful

Reconcile/ ratify the difference between non-GAAP and comparable GAAP measure

Purpose of using non-GAAP measure

IFRS requires following to be disclosed for using non IFRS measures

Relevance of such measure

Reconcile the difference between non IFRS and most comparable IFRS measure

Here is an example of non-GAAP measure from which you will have quite the idea.

A company is downsizing and expensing much on it. They may exclude these expenses and show more information on operations for paint a good picture.

7: Describe accounting methods (choices and estimates) that could be used to manage earnings, cash flow, and balance sheet items

There are various ways by which management can change results and show better results in their financial reports. Through these methods they can affect the balance sheet, income statement and cash flows.

Some of these methods are used to gear up a below normal performance and other can reduce the results.

Choices affecting balance sheet: We must be looking in

- Revenue recognition.

- Inventory management.
- Accrual accounting
- Deferred tax assets.
- Depreciation.
- Capitalization of expenses.

Revenue recognition: It means management is recognizing revenues early or delaying them according to their need.

For example, we have a huge order to export goods at the end of a period. We need to recognize the earnings when the title and responsibilities of ordered goods have been transferred. But in order to make things look better management decides to recognize the revenues before the end of the period (and before the transfer of responsibility) they are influencing the revenues for the current period.

Inventory: How the management is recording cost of goods sold and ending inventory in the accounts.

We have three methods, **FIFO** first in first out, weighted average cost, and LIFO method last in first out.

When prices are going up use of FIFO gives us out of dated cost of goods sold but a better inventory in hand (inventory value is according to current market prices). This makes the balance sheet look better.

By using weighted average method, the cost of goods sold is somewhat closer to the current fair value but the balance sheet is not as close to the current market value of inventory (as it was with the use of FIFO). Management has opportunity here to engineer the balance sheet according to their need.

LIFO is not permitted under IFRS so let`s not discuss it here as we have discussed it in detail before. I think we got the idea how inventory method can be used by management in their favor.

Accrual accounting: It is a method of reporting current period activity as opposed to current period cash. It means revenues and expenses should be recognized when they occur irrespective to cash may or may not change hands.

Management can use this approach in their favor to manipulate results. When a firm sold the goods, they have receivables. They need to maintain a provision for bad debts and fair value of collectibles. These two items are subject to the judgment of management.

Deferred tax assets: After experiencing a loss, the management creates an account of deferred tax asset in their balance sheet. When they will be in profit

They will use that deferred tax asset to reduce their tax bill. This is true for a startup companies and the successful companies who hit a loss accidently. But what if a company is in decline and will be getting out of business in next four or five year they may not use their entire deferred tax asset. This is also a subjective approach and is on management`s discretion.

Depreciation methods: It is an allocation of the cost of a long-lived asset to the several years.

There are three major methods.

- Straight line.
- Accelerated
- Activity based.

And we also have to estimate salvage value.

The choice of depreciation method and estimates about salvage value depends on management. The different choice may lead towards different results.

Capitalization: It means firm has to decide whether the expense they made is going to give them benefit in one year or in multiple years. Sometimes management delays the current expenses by capitalizing to show better earnings in current period.

Accounting choices to influence the statement of cash flow
Statement of cash flow has three parts

- CFO, operating cash flows.
- CFI, cash flows from investment activities.
- CFF, cash flow from financing activities.

Within cash flow statement, CFO is of most importance to check earnings of the firm. With respect to accruals and depreciation, cash flows are less likely to be manipulated.

First of all, we need to check relationship between net income and operating cash flow.

If amount of cash generated in a period > net income, we have good quality earnings and financial reports.

If amount of cash generated in a period < net income, we have bad quality earnings and financial reports.

When cash inflow is far low from net earnings it means management did something to report higher earnings than actual reality.

The company management knows lower inflow from operation will look bad, they also use some methods to raise cash inflow. The most common way of doing this is managing account payables. What if management wants to show more cash in hand by delaying payment to their supplier? They will be raising account payables but cash position would be higher. They can fool us if we only see at cash position and ignore payables.

Sometimes management decides to show improved cash flow by **misclassifying items** from investing or financing activities. In this method they bring inflow items in CFO. Sometimes management constructs a complex transaction/agreement to confuse user which is also a bad sign.

8: Describe accounting warning signs and methods for detecting manipulation of information in financial reports

In this LOS we will be looking at

- Revenues,
- Inventory,
- Capitalization,
- Relationship between net income and cash flow,
- Fourth quarter earnings
- Non-recurring entries.

Revenues: This is the item which is the number one source of manipulation. So, we have to look at this item first. First of all we need to look at the notes for management policies regarding revenue recognition, rebates etc. Any suspicious entry here would be a bad start

If a company has outperformed comparative to their peers and competitors we need to check it. Does this performance is achieved through superior management, superior product or through manipulation.

If the firm has outperformed deviated from its historical trends we need to check for a reasonable explanation.

After that we need to check ratios like receivables turnover, days sales outstanding, asset turnover and compare them to the industry norms.

Inventory: The firms who holds inventory has significant opportunities to manipulate it. We must check and compare inventory figure with industry norms and the company`s own historical trends. Anything unusual must be checked for reasonable explanation.

Inventory turnover ratios must also be checked. A declining inventory turnover might indicate threat of obsolescence. We should compare it with industry norms and the company`s historical trends and or a reasonable explanation.

Capitalization: It also means deferring of costs. First of all, check the notes regarding policies relating to capitalization. Compare these policies with industry norms. If difference appears check out asset turnover and profitability ratios for comparability.

Relationship between net income and cash flow: Cash inflows plays very critical role for a company to perform well and even to survive. When a firm is aggressively capitalizing cost (means delaying cost as expense) they are showing higher income for current period. Same results can also be achieved by aggressive accrual accounting. If cash is not coming in despite higher earnings it must get the analyst into suspicion. We need to calculate percentage of cash inflow with respect to income (cash inflow/ income) over a number of years to see the trends. If cash inflow percentage declines it's a red flag and analyst must demand or seek further investigation.

Fourth quarter earnings: we need to look at 4th quarter earnings. Are they match with previous quarter`s earnings or not? (Of course we must consider the element of seasonality).

Non-recurring or one-off items: We need to look closely for non-recurring items if they recur again and again and vice versa. For example, a huge cash inflow from non-recurring item, stated into income from operations and an expense stated into non-recurring expense but coming into accounts several times.

Learning Module 11
Financial Analysis Techniques

1: Describe tools and techniques used in financial analysis, including their uses and limitations

There are several tools and techniques which are used to convert financial statements into those formats which can be easily analyzed. These are ratio analysis, common size analysis, graphical analysis, regression analysis etc.

These tools are very importance when companies are not compatible because of different locations or maybe they operate in different industries.

Ratio analysis benefits: Ratio analysis is used for

- Internal and external comparison.
- To project future earnings and cash flow.
- To evaluate a company's financial flexibility (ability to obtain cash) to meet its obligations and to grow even in case of difficult financial circumstance.
- To measure the performance of a company's management.
- To look at how the company or the industry is changing over time.
- To compare company with their peer companies or relevant industry benchmarks.

Limitation of ratios: 1. They are not useful in isolation. They are only useful when they are combined with an overall understanding of the company the company's industry and the macroeconomic environment.

1. Ratio analysis is also not useful for big companies that have

multiple sources of income from entirely different industries. Because of the complexity of the big company, relevant benchmarks won't be available.

1. Analysis based on small subset of ratios might not be reliable because one set of financial ratios might indicate a certain level of performance but another set of ratios on the same company might indicate that that performance level is not sustainable.

2. Ratios calculated from financial reports build on differing accounting standards may not be immediately comparable. (Accounting treatments differs in inventory evaluation, appreciation and off-balance sheet items.)

Common size analysis: Common size is all about expressing financial data or entire financial statements relative to a single item.

<u>Vertical common size</u> balance sheets base everything relative to total assets. So total assets would be marked in the report as a hundred percent and everything else is expressed as a percentage of that total assets figure. For example, percentage of cash $= \dfrac{\text{cash}}{\text{total asset}} \times 100$

The benefits:
We can determine

- The company's financing sources. and
- How does the company's balance sheet differ from the industry norm.

<u>Vertical common size income statements</u> are very similar to a vertical common size balance sheet. In vertical common size income statement everything is calculated as percentage of total revenues. For example, Gross profit percentage $= \dfrac{\text{Gross profit}}{\text{sales}} \times 100$.

Vertical common size reports both balance sheet and income statement are useful to an analyst performing a cross sectional analysis. With cross sectional analysis we're comparing some metric of one company to that same metric from another company or to an industry benchmark.

For example, if one company has shown receivables on their vertical common size balance sheet thirty two percent of total assets but another company or all of the companies in the industry are below ten percent.

We need to know what this company is doing differently. This requires more investigation.

<u>Horizontal common size statements</u> state everything relative to a base year.

For example, if the total assets in the first year are a hundred twenty million dollars and in the next year they have total assets on the hundred and thirty million dollars.

The first year will be shown as a hundred percent with the second-year show is a hundred eight-point three percent. This format is useful for answering questions like how the relative position of the company is changing and how was their management of receivables and payable changing over time.

Horizontal common size statements are useful for trend analysis.

XYZ corp. LTD

Income statement

For the year ended 31Dec.2xx9 Vertical common size income statement

Sales	1000	(1000/1000)x10000=	100%
COGS	600	600/1000)x100 (600/1000)x100=	60%
GP	400	(400/1000)x100(400/1000)x100=	40%
Operating exp	40	(40/1000)x100=	4%
Admin exp	30	(30/1000)x100=	3%
Tax Expense	10	(10/1000)x100=	1%
Net profit	320	(320/1000)x100=	32%

XYZ corp. LTD
   Balance sheet
   As on 31Dec.2xx9

Year	2xx6	2xx7	2xx8	Horizontal common size balance sheet taking 2xx6 as base year		
				2xx6 (%)	2xx7 (%)	2xx8 (%)
Assets						
Cash and cash equivalents	100	120	140	(100/100)x100= 100%	(120/100)x100 = 120%	140
Account receivables	80	90	100	(80/80) x100 =100	**(90/80)x100 =112.5**	125
Inventory	200	210	220	100	105	110
PP&E	1000	1000	1000	100	100	100
Total assets	**1380**	**1420**	**1460**	**100**	**102.89**	**105.79**
Liabilities						
Account payables	100	105	110	100	105	110
Interest payable	50	55	60	100	110	120
long term debt	700	730	760	100	104.2857143	108.5714
total liabilities	**850**	**890**	**930**	**100**	**104.71**	**109.41**
common equity	530	530	530	100	100	100
Total liabilities & Equity	**1380**	**1420**	**1460**	**100**	**102.89%**	**105.79**

Graphical analysis: Graphical analysis is building visual representations of financial information to aid in the understanding comparison or explanation of the company's financial performance. Some examples of graphical analysis tools are stocked bar graphs, pie charts and line graphs. Each is useful in their own way for expressing information over different time periods and emphasizing different areas.

Regression analysis: Regression analysis is all about discovering a statistical relationship between two variables. (Details are not included in CFA curriculum)

Common example is sales to GDP. Can we draw a significantly consistent relationship between how company sales changes in relation to real GDP.

2: Calculate and interpret activity, liquidity, solvency, and profitability ratios

In this LOS we have to classify these ratios, calculate them and also interpret them.

We have four classifications of ratios.

1. Activity ratios: 2. Liquidity ratios 3. Solvency ratios 4. Profitability ratios

Note: These classifications are not mutually exclusive.

Activity ratios

Activity ratios are also called asset utilization ratios or operating efficiency ratios. These ratios measure firm's ability to manage their assets. We have following ratios in this category.

Receivable turnover ratio: How efficiently a firm control receivable is measured by **receivable turnover ratio**.

Receivable turnover ratio = Annual sales/ average receivables.

This ratio should be closer to industry norms.

One thing must be remembered here is that whenever we use balance sheet data with income statement or cash flow data in a ratio, the balance sheet figure must be taken as average by adding opening and ending balances and divided by 2.

Number of days sales are outstanding or average collection period: It is the average number of days taken by the customers to pay to the firm.

No. of days sales outstanding = 365/ receivable turnover

This ratio should be close to industry norms. If it is too high it means the firm is not collecting cash easily (inefficiency). A too low this ratio shows a very strict credit policy which might be affecting sales or the firm is collecting cash very efficiently.

Inventory turnover ratio= Cost of goods sold/ average inventory

It measures firm's efficiency in inventory management and its processing. It tells how many times the firm has sold its inventory completely (theoretically).

Days inventory in hand = 365/ inventory turnover

It tells us how many days a firm takes to process its inventory. Again, these (Inventory turnover and Days inventory in hand) should be close to industry norms. A higher inventory turnover ratio means lesser days inventory in hand. It might indicate a highly effective inventory management or the company is not holding enough stock and is potentially on the verge of shortages and falling sales revenue. Analyst must see revenues growth to assess the explanation. A higher (or same as industry) growth with high turnover means effective inventory management and vice versa. A lower inventory turnover means higher number of days inventory in hand may indicate that there is too much capital is tied up and high processing time. It means inventory could be getting obsolete. The cost of goods sold may not be according to current circumstances.

Payable turnover ratio = purchases/ average payables: It means how many times company pays its payables completely (theoretically).

Number of days of payables= 365/ payable turnover ratio

These two should be close to industry norms. A relatively higher payables turnover (which would mean a relatively lower number of days payables are outstanding) the company might not be effectively taking advantage of credit facilities made available to them or they might be taking advantage of early payment discounts. We must look at the liquidity ratios to get proper understanding. If company has better liquidity ratios but higher days payable (lower payable turnover) it means they are taking advantage of available credit facilities. If liquidity position is bad with lower payable turnover they might be having trouble with cash generation.

Working capital turn over = Total sales/ average working capital. Working capital is the difference between current assets and current liabilities.

It tells us how efficiently the company is turning their working capital investment into sales revenue. It indicates how much revenue the company is generating per dollar of working capital investment. For example, if working capital turnover is 5, it means for every dollar of working capital we generate five dollars of sales revenue. A zero or negative of this ratio is not useable.

The fixed asset turnover = Sales revenue by/ Average net fixed assets

It tells us how efficiently investment in fixed assets is being turned into sales revenue.

Interpretation: Higher figure would indicate efficient use of fixed assets. A lower number may indicate inefficiency in business because it requires a large capital investment. Or it is a newborn company that has not yet reached at its full capacity.

Total asset turnover = Sales revenue / average total assets

It tells us how efficiently the company is generating revenue from their assets.

Interpretation: A higher figure indicates that the company is effectively or efficiently utilizing their assets to generate revenue. Lower figure would indicate inefficiencies or the firm is in very capital-intensive business.

Liquidity ratios

Liquidity ratios measure a company's ability to meet its short-term obligations.

We have 3 major liquidity ratios, the current ratio, the quick ratio and the cash ratio.

Current ratio= Current assets /current liabilities.

Quick ratio= Liquid assets / current liabilities. Where, Liquid assets = cash+ marketable sec. + receivables

Cash ratio = (cash + marketable securities) / current liabilities.

Interpretations

A current ratio of one indicates that the company's current assets are equals the dollar value of their current liabilities. So, the short-term obligations are just covered. A ratio less than one means that the company is relying on operating profit to meet short term obligations because current assets are not enough.

Same interpretation is for following ratios too.

Quick ratio is more realistic approach about our ability to convert certain current assets into cash. Pre-payments for example might be included in the current assets of a company but would be are very difficult to turn into cash. Same is the case with inventory. So, we exclude these two in quick ratio to have more meaningful results.

With cash ratio we are more conservative about the asset`s ability to meet short-term obligations. We only include most liquid assets. We only include cash and marketable securities the company has right now to pay their short term obligations.

Other liquidity ratios: The defensive interval and the cash conversion cycle.

Defensive interval = (cash + marketable securities + receivables)/ average daily expenditures

It is a measure of how long the company can continue paying its liabilities with current assets assuming no new inflows.

For example, a defensive interval of 40 means the company can survive the current pace for 40 days without getting any cash inflow. Higher number indicates greater liquidity.

Cash conversion cycle = {(days sales outstanding) +days inventory in hand) – (Number of days of payables)}

It is the time company takes to turn a product into cash (from inventory to receivable to cash collection).

A shorter time means greater liquidity. It should be compared with industry norms.

Solvency ratios:

Solvency ratios measure a company's ability to meet longer term obligations. This category is most relevant to analysts interested in a company's financial leverage and their ability to service long term debt.

Solvency ratios typically have two categories.

1. Debt ratios 2. Coverage ratios

Debt ratios

Debt to equity = Total debt / total equity.

This ratio compares the debt side of the capital structure to the equity side. It shows how much debt a company is using to finance its assets in comparison to equity. A higher figure would indicate a less solvent company.

Debt to assets ratio= total debt / total assets.

This ratio compares the company's debt position to the value of their total assets. It tells us the percentage of total assets financed by debt (all liabilities). A higher ratio indicates weak solvency.

Debt to capital ratio= Total debt / (total debt + shareholders equity).

Total debt means all interest bearing short and long-term debt. Equity includes common stock and preferred stock. It shows how much of capital is financed by debt. A higher ratio indicates weak solvency.

Financial leverage= Average total assets / average total equity.

A higher ratio here indicates the company is using a higher proportion of debt to finance their assets which indicates risk.

Coverage ratios

There are two major coverage ratios, interest coverage ratio and the fixed charge coverage ratio.

Interest coverage ratio= EBIT/interest payment

EBIT is earning before interest and taxes. It measures how many times a company's earnings before interest and tax covers their interest obligations.

A higher number is desirable here because it indicates that the earnings are quite bigger than interest payment. A lower of this ratio means they have difficulty in payment of interest.

Fixed charge coverage = (EBIT + lease payments) / (interest expense plus lease payments).

It tells us how well the company's fixed outflows are covered by their earning. A higher ratio indicates the company is in a better position and vice versa.

Profitability ratios

Profitability ratios measure the overall performance of the firm in terms of revenues, assets, capital and equity.

Before the profitability ratios we need a good understanding of the structure of the income statement.

Net sales revenue - cost of goods sold = gross profit.

Gross profit -operating expenses = operating profit EBIT = earnings before interest and taxes

EBIT- interest = earnings before tax= EBT

EBT- taxes = earnings after tax.

Earnings after tax – other items = net income before dividends.

Total capital = long term debt + short term debt + common equity + preferred equity.

Some analysts may use total assets for total capital if they want to include things like accounts payable.

No let's look at the profitability ratio.

We have two categories of profitability ratios

1. Ratios based on the company's sales revenue 2. Ratios based on capital invested.

Ratios based on the company's sales revenue

Gross profit margin = gross profit / revenues.

Gross profit margin indicates the number of sales left over after counting for the cost of goods sold. It is a comparison of Gross profit with sales. A higher gross profit margin indicates company's ability to charge a higher price for a product they can manufacture for a lower cost and vice versa. Gross profit margin also helps the management in cost control.

Operating profit margin = Operating profit / sales revenues.

We know that operating profit is gross profit minus operating costs. While analyzing operating profit margin it's a custom to compare the trend of operating Margin with gross margin.

If operating profit margin is improving faster than gross profit margin then the company may be getting more efficient to bring down the operating cost.

Pretax margin = earnings before tax / sales revenue.

This is another measure of profitability. An analyst should be careful to consider whether the item driving a change in pretax margin is likely to continue into the future or if it's a onetime event (due to non-recurring items).

Ratios based on capital invested

Return on assets =Net income / average total assets.

It tells us how much income the company has earned per dollar of assets. This is a better measure of how they performed by taking their size into consideration. The main problem with this ratio is that net income is a return for only equity holders (both common and preferred) but for most companies, assets are financed by both equity and debt.

To eliminate this drawback and account for debt holder's profitability an analyst might use operating return on assets, calculated as

ROA= (Net income + interest expense (1-tax rate)} / average total assets.

Return on total capital= EBIT/Average total capital

Total capital is short and long-term debt and common and preferred equity. In this ratio we measure the return on per dollar of capital invested. A very low of this ratio from industry norms should alarm the analyst.

Return on equity (or return on total equity) = Net income / average total equity.

This ratio focuses on the equity holders including preferred equity. It should also be according to industry norms. A very low of this ratio must concern analyst.

Return on common equity = Net income – preferred dividends)/average common equity

While

Net income – preferred dividends = income available to common stock holders.

This ratio measures the return just to the common shareholders and compares that figure to the capital invested by just the common shareholders.

3: Describe relationships among ratios and evaluate a company using ratio analysis

Let's have an example to relate ratios and company evaluation.

Sample balance sheet

Year	Current	
Assets	000$	000$
Cash and equivalent	50	40
Trade receivables	70	60
inventory	210	200
total current assets	**330**	**300**
Property plant and equipment	2000	2000
Accumulated depreciation	300	295
Net property plant and equipment	1700	1720
Total assets	**2030**	**2020**

Liabilities

Trade payables	114	113
Current portion of long term debt	70	65
Short term debt	130	125
Total current liabilities	**314**	**295**
Long term debt	590	610
Deferred tax	116	110
Common stock at par	260	260
Additional paid up capital	500	500
Retained earnings	250	245
Total shareholders' equity	1010	1005
Total liabilities and equity	**2030**	**2020**

Sample income statement

Year	Current	previous
Sales	10000	**9500**
Cost of goods sold	9000	8600
Gross profit	1000	900
Operating expenses	560	540
EBIT	440	360
Interest expense	40	35
EBT	400	325
Taxes	55	52
Net income	345	273
Common dividend	245	173

Ratios	Current	Previous	
Current ratio	1.05	1.016949153	1.1
Quick ratio	0.38	0.338983051	1
cash ratio	0.1592357	0.169491525	0.7
inventory turnover	43.902439	41.95121951	42
days inventory in hand	8.3138889	8.700581395	8

receivable turnover	153.84615	146.1538462
days sales outstanding	2.3725	2.497368421

Now let's look at what these ratios are telling us about this company.

Firstly, in terms of the <u>current ratio,</u>

The current ratio is increasing which suggests that current assets are increasing relative to current liabilities. Meaning that the company is improving its liquidity position. Moreover, it is also close to industry benchmark.

But the quick ratio doesn't look so good. Although it has increased slightly but still very low from industry bench mark. It tells us that we do not have sufficient more liquid assets.

If we have only two ratios it is fair to comment that the company`s liquidity is not good and inventory is misleading its current ratio.

No if we bring in the days sales outstanding figures we just calculated we can see a decline from 2.4 days to 2.3 days. This is suggesting that the company is collecting cash on their receivables a bit quicker than they were before which is a positive sign but it is still greater than industry.

Days inventory in hand is also improving and is very close to industry norms.

Putting all of that together it looks like although this company's inventory and receivable ratios are good but their liquidity position is actually weakening.

4: Demonstrate the application of DuPont analysis of return on equity and calculate and interpret effects of changes in its components

DuPont analysis: It is a method used to analyze a company's return on equity. In this we can use algebra to break the simple return on equity formula and find out what is driving return on equity.

The basic formula: return on equity= Net income / average equity.

If we multiply above and below the line by sales revenue and rearrange it, we come up with following formula.

$$ROE = \left\{ \frac{\text{Net income}}{\text{Sale}} \right\} \times \left(\frac{\text{sales}}{\text{Average equity}} \right)$$

And again, by total assets we end up with a formula that looks like this.

$$ROE = \left\{ \frac{\text{Netincome}}{\text{sale}} \right\} \times \left\{ \frac{\text{Sales}}{\text{Total assets}} \right\} \times \left\{ \frac{\text{Total assets}}{\text{Average equity}} \right\}$$

The first part net income over sales is the company's net profit margin, the second piece sales over assets is the company's asset turnover and assets over equity is the company's leverage ratio also known as the equity multiplier.

One important thing to realize here is that if we combine these first two parts we end up with net income over assets which is return on assets. Now in terms of interpretation we have looked at these metrics to some extent already.

Net profit margin measures the company's ability to generate profits from their ordinary business activity. A higher number here indicates the company in a good position in their industry.

Asset turnover gives us a measure of how the company is able to generate sales from their assets. This is a valuable comparison mechanism that can be used to compare companies of different sizes. Again, a higher figure indicates a better performing company.

With financial leverage we're looking at the company's financial risk and solvency.

Comparing the company's assets to their equity position is just the same as comparing liabilities plus equity to the equity position. It is a measure of what proportion of the capital structure this company holds on the liability side. Higher number here indicates a company with more obligations, more risk and more chance of insolvency.

DuPont analysis can be extended by further breaking down this first term the net profit margin. For this part we multiply by EBT/EBT and EBIT/EBIT and re arrange to end up with a form that looks like this.

ROE= {Net income/ EBT} x {EBT/ EBIT} x {EBIT/ Sales} x {sales/Average assets} x {Average assets/ average equity}

Now we already know these last two components are asset turnover and the leverage ratio so those are interpreted the same as we had before.

This first term Net income over earnings before tax is known as the tax burden. Earnings before tax over EBIT is also known as the company's interest burden which gives us an indication of how the company's interest expense changes relative to earnings.

The term EBIT over sales is called the EBIT margin. This figure tells us how much the company`s revenues comes from their operating profit, so how much is based on their everyday business activity.

5: Describe the uses of industry-specific ratios used in financial analysis

Specific ratios

These ratios give us general idea but there are other specific ratios related to specific industry. Financial services companies, for example, are supposed to follow some specific regulations. For these types of companies, ratios like <u>capital adequacy</u> under monetary reserve requirement are important.

In the service industry we might interested in net income per employee or sales per employee ratios.

In the retail industry <u>sales per square foot is important</u>.

Coefficient of variation metrics

We can measure riskiness of different financial statements items like coefficient of variation of sales (CV sales $= \dfrac{\text{Standard deviation of sales}}{\text{mean sales}}$) and CV of net income (

$$\text{CV of net income} = \dfrac{\text{SD net income}}{\text{mean net income}}$$) etc.

6: Describe how ratio analysis and other techniques can be used to model and forecast earnings

If sales revenues forecasts are given analyst can use historic data and trend analysis to forecast certain elements of financial statements like gross profit.

Forecasts are generally a distribution of possible outcomes (and not a single point estimates). In forecast building the techniques like sensitivity analysis, (analysis of changes in inputs), Scenario analysis, Assimilation are used.

Sensitivity analysis: Sensitivity analysis is based on what if conditions. For example, what would happen to gross profit if cost of goods sold changes by 1 percent.

Scenario analysis: Analyzing the effect of a change of a set of input variables.

Assimilation: Taking a distribution of inputs to yield a distribution of outputs.

Learning Module 12

Introduction to Financial Statement Modeling

1: Demonstrate the development of a sales-based pro forma company model

Using a proforma model that focuses on sales, one can accurately predict the future performance of a company by forecasting its sales revenues. This model is useful for making informed decisions, particularly in capital budgeting, financial planning, and operational strategies. It makes certain assumptions about sales growth, cost of goods sold, and other factors.

Construction of Pro Forma Income Statement

This involves the following four steps: revenue forecasting, COGS forecasting, other operating expenses forecasting, and non-operating items forecasting.

We consider the company`s market share, company`s historical growth trends, and rate and growth relative to GDP to forecast these items. Consider following a very simple example.

We use single estimate of growth rate and use it to forecast future item. For example we use 5% for sales and use it for future sales revenues.

To estimate future cash flows we need to make some assumptions of uses and sources of cash.

By building multi-period forecast we end up as follows

Income and cashflow projections

	2x10 current	2x11	2x12	2x13
Sale @4%	1200	1248	1297.9	1349.8
Less COGS @5%	600	630	661.5	694.58
Less opearting expenses@3%	200	206	212.18	218.55
Net income	400	412	424.24	436.72
Opening cash@2%	200	204	208.08	212.24
Net income	400	412	424.24	436.72
Non cash items (working capital)@75% of sales	900	936	973.44	1012.4
Ending cash	**1500**	**1552**	**1605.8**	**1661.3**

2: Explain how behavioral factors affect analyst forecasts and recommend remedial actions for analyst biases

Behavioral bias

Following are the main behavioral biases;

a. **Overconfidence bias:** Overconfidence bias is the tendency to make erroneous and inaccurate assessments of our talents, intellect, or aptitude.

It has two further types

i. Prediction overconfidence: Prediction overconfidence refers to an investor's tendency to make overly specific predictions with a very narrow range.

ii. Certainty overconfidence: Overconfidence in one's capacity to select the next big stock with 100% certainty (or higher probability) is known as certainty overconfidence.

Effects: Overconfident investors may overestimate expected gains while underestimating potential risks.

Investors may opt to invest their money into poorly diversified portfolios, placing themselves at risk of losing a large sum of money.

<u>How to detect and avoid:</u> Consider the ramifications. Consider the repercussions while making a decision. Challenge yourself while assessing your abilities. Maintain an open mind. Consider your blunders and never ignore them. Pay attention to what others have to say.

Self-Control Bias: When people prioritize instant gratification above long-term goals, they develop self-control bias. It's an emotional human-behavioral tendency in which people fail to act in pursuit of their long-term overall goals owing to a lack of self-control in the short term.

Effects: As a result of investor's incapacity to save for the future, investors may take on excessive stock market risk and borrow too much money at even higher rates in order to generate higher returns.

Self-control bias may result in an asset allocation mismatch, as well as investors losing sight of basic financial principles.

<u>*How to detect and avoid:*</u> Investors should be disciplined, make personal budgets, and plan their investments. These plans must be evaluated on a regular intervals.

a. <u>*Conservatism bias:*</u> Conservative bias is defined as holding on to old beliefs or ideas while accepting new information that contradicts or upsets those beliefs or notions with hesitancy. People have a tendency to overestimate their own prediction based on old information in general and underestimate new information. As a result, incorrect conclusions are reached and inadequate solutions to new problems are implemented.

Implications / effects of conservative biases on financial decision-making: Even with the availability of new information, the investor may be slow to update his investment forecast.

Sometimes, investors may choose to stay with old beliefs rather than deal with the stress of updating their beliefs on the basis of new information.

For example, an investor may buy a security in an oil and gas exploration company because it has discovered some new oil wells. After a few weeks, the company discloses that the newly discovered wells do not provide sufficient crude oil. If the investor sticks to his or her initial assessment of the firm and fails to adjust their assessment based on fresh facts, he is subject to conservative bias.

How to Recognize and Overcome the Conservatism Bias

- **Seek Professional Advice:** To avoid conservatism bias an investor must consult other specialists to assist them in making financial decisions. In this way the same available information can be interpreted in a different way.

- Do adequate analysis and weigh the new information properly. After the deep analysis, the investor should act quickly as time is very important in investment decision-making.

a. _Confirmation bias:_ The propensity to appreciate or recognize information that confirms one's present ideas while dismissing evidence that contradicts them is known as confirmation bias. It happens when someone rationalizes their beliefs in order to ease cognitive stress.

Implications/effects of Confirmation bias on financial decision-making:

- An investor can wrongly focus on the positive sides of an investment opportunity while ignoring the negative points about it.
- While just focusing on positive news, the investor may under-diversify the portfolio, which may result in more losses than it may produce.

How to recognize and overcome the _Confirmation bias_

This bias can be mitigated by finding out the contradictory piece of information.

By analyzing the investment opportunity on the basis of different perspectives can help to reduce this bias.

Representative Bias: When we interpret new knowledge as a duplicate or representative of old experience. While new information may appear to be similar to previously classified information, the two sets of information may actually be completely different.

There are two types of representative bias

- Base rate neglect: The frequency of an occurrence in a wider population is neglected in favor of specific knowledge.
- Sample size neglect: In this situation, investors make the error of assuming that tiny sample sizes correctly represent populations.

Implications/effects of **representative bias** on financial decision-making:
A Financial forecast is mostly dependent on limited sample size or individual, unique data as a consequence of representational bias.

An investor will not tend to take stress to update the belief which will cause losses.

How to recognize and overcome the _representative bias_

Learn more about statistics and logical reasoning to avoid representativeness bias, and ask others to point out situations where you may be focusing too much on representativeness.

3: Explain how the competitive position of a company based on Porter's five forces analysis affects prices and costs

A framework developed by Peter called "Porter's Five Forces" can be used to determine a competitive environment.

According to Porter there are following five determinants of competition in an industry:

Threat of entry: If there is less threat of new entry, the existing firms would hold significant pricing power and can earn economic profits. The barriers to new entry can be huge initial costs, economies of scale, or governmental restrictions. The analyst should carefully examine these factors.

Rivalry among existing firms: The existing firms also compete with each other for market share. When there are more firms of the same size in an industry, the competition would be tough, and there would be less pricing power.

Bargaining power of supplier: If the raw material suppliers have more bargaining power, they will raise the prices, lower the quality, and reduce the quantity. Bargaining power of supplier increases if there are limited numbers of suppliers exist in the market.

Bargaining power of buyers: The buyers can also exert pressure on the businesses to reduce prices, increase quality, and better after-sales services. All these elements reduce profitability. Sometimes, governments also pressure the firms to reduce the prices and increase the quality of healthcare and transportation types of businesses.

Threat of substitutes: The availability of substitutes increases the price elasticity, and the firms cannot charge high prices. Moreover, the firms can feel if they charge a high price, there will be more firms entering the market, which will take away their share. This factor also limits their pricing power.

4: Explain how to forecast industry and company sales and costs when they are subject to price inflation or deflation

Inflation and deflation affect the industry and the specific company in many ways, and forecasting this effect is challenging. However, these forecasts are necessary for the analyst to have deep insight into the future of the company and industry. Inflation and deflation affect the input costs, pricing strategies, and eventually the sales revenues.

We need to divide this section into the following parts;

Sales in an Inflation Scenario (Industry and company

Inflation affects the demand of the industry. With a negative slope of the demand curve, the increase in the prices mainly decreases the aggregate demand, especially when there are alternative products/services available. Therefore, with an increase in the cost of 10 percent and subsequently companies increasing their prices by 10 percent, their gross profit margin will remain the same, but sales will decrease. The ability of companies to pass the price hike to the customers is another issue and depends on the industry to industry.

Revenue forecasts for the company heavily depend on the price elasticity of demand for that product. Different rates of inflation affect the companies in different countries. Market structure, competitive position of the company, and pricing strategies are important factors to consider when forecasting the company's sales revenues. If the demand is inelastic, the price increase will cause the revenues to increase. If there is elastic demand, their revenues will decrease with increased prices. With equal elastic demand $(E=1)$ there will be no revenue increase with price changes. If the company is export-oriented and there is inflation in the foreign markets, the exports will be costlier for the customers. Pricing strategy is also an essential factor. The companies might want to transfer the inflation to the customers to maintain the gross profit margin, or they might want to accept a lower profit margin to capture the market.

Sales in a Deflation Scenario (Industry and Company)

With deflation, the decrease in the general price level increases the consumers' purchasing power, which might increase the aggregate demand depending on the industry type and other factors. Companies are not prepared for this increase in demand, and there is a shortage of products/services in the market. Sometimes the companies (especially coordinated cartels) do not want to reduce the prices in order to avoid a price war. This is true, especially when the companies face equal elastic demand.

The company's pricing strategy is critical in deflationary situations. Lowering manufacturing costs and other strategies is always a solid method to retain long-term profitability in the face of declining pricing. Sales revenues will decrease as prices decline. In this situation, expanding into new markets with stable pricing may help to offset revenue declines. People anticipate reduced costs for all items when the general price level falls. A corporation will lose the market if it fails to meet these expectations.

Costs in an Inflation Scenario (industry and company)

It's essential to consider the key factors that impact production costs in an industry, such as raw material availability, energy prices, and wage rates. Implementing long-term contracts with raw material suppliers and workers and hedging strategies can help safeguard industries from rising production costs when there is anticipation or occurrence of inflation. The market structure directly impacts how costs are transferred to consumers.

It is essential to comprehend the company's operations, financial details, and pricing strategies to predict its costs in an inflationary environment. The company's ability to transfer the cost onto the consumer is contingent upon its competitive position in the industry.

Improving efficiency is a practical approach to reducing costs. Alternative inputs may prove advantageous.

Costs in a Deflation Scenario (Industry and Company)

When industries are grappling with deflationary pressures and struggling to sustain their profit margins. Understanding the breakdown of costs, such as fixed and variable costs, is crucial for conducting a thorough analysis. When operating in deflationary environments, negotiating with suppliers and workers can be a wise strategy to establish new prices and wages. Reducing expenses to sustain profitability amidst decreasing revenues can also be beneficial. When prices start to decline, it can lead to price wars that hurt the industry.

In the event of deflationary pressure, companies require strategic planning, operational efficiency, and supply chain factors to reduce costs. Contract renegotiations with suppliers and employees and working with the cost structure (variable and fixed) are also crucial.

5: Explain considerations in the choice of an explicit forecast horizon and an analyst's choices in developing projections beyond the short-term forecast horizon

Factors that impact the selection of a forecast time horizon

Several factors influence the selection of a forecast time horizon.

The time horizon of the investment strategy is determined by the **type of strategy** being implemented.

Industrial sector **Cyclicality** is an essential factor to consider. When analyzing a cyclical company, it is vital to consider a longer time horizon that encompasses mid-cycle revenues and other industry indicators.

Factors specific to the company: There are certain aspects that set a company apart. Events such as acquisitions and mergers can have an impact on the forecasted time horizon.

Employer selection for the analyst: Sometimes the analyst has to consider the employer's preference when selecting the forecast horizon.

Looking ahead to the future

Long-term forecasts are utilized to mitigate short-term disruptions and gauge normalized earnings.

Typically, beginning with sales revenues is a solid starting point.

It is crucial to thoroughly assess the company's terminal value by taking into account various factors such as free cash flow, long-term growth rate, regulation and technological changes, and macroeconomic conditions.

Did you love *CFA Level 1 Financial Statement Analysis*? Then you should read *CFA 2025: Level 1 Fixed Income*[1] by M. Imran Ahsan!

If you want to learn CFA easily and with less time, you have the right book. If you think Fixed income is diffcult, just read this book. It will change your perception.

Many books are available in the market for the same purpose and they are good. The main quality of this book which distinguishes it from others is this book covers whole syllabus in very precise and comprehensive manner. This book makes difficult concepts easy and understandable.

We believe in simplicity and conciseness. This book is a complete and a comprehensive guide with simple language.

---

1. https://books2read.com/u/4NL1RW

2. https://books2read.com/u/4NL1RW

You can learn the complete Fixed Income material in just one week with the help of this book.

Also by M. Imran Ahsan

ACCA
AACA: Business & Technology

CFA level 1
CFA 2025: Level 1 corporate Issuers
CFA Level 1 Financial Statement Analysis
CFA level 1: 2025 Equity Investments
CFA 2025: Level 1 Fixed Income
Economics for CFA 2024: level 1 in just one week
CFA Level 1: Derivatives and Alternative Investments
CFA 2025: level 1 Portfolio management

Investment series
Corporate Finance: A Beginner's Guide
Fixed Income Securities: A Beginner's Guide to Understand, Invest
and Evaluate Fixed Income Securities

About the Author

I am a PhD scholar and is a university lecturer for more than 11 years. I have been teaching Finance and Economics at various levels.

As an instructor I believe in simplicity, comprehensivity and in conciseness. I believe in smart kind of hard work. It means you should use your time efficiently to achieve optimal goals with limited time and efforts.

www.ingramcontent.com/pod-product-compliance
Lightning Source LLC
Chambersburg PA
CBHW021004180726
47993CB00017B/700